When Did I Stop Being Barbie & Become Mrs. Potato Head?

When Did I Stop Being Barbie & Become Mrs. Potato Head?

LEARNING TO EMBRACE THE WOMAN YOU'VE BECOME

MARY PIERCE

GRAND RAPIDS, MICHIGAN 49530 USA

ZONDERVAN™

When Did I Stop Being Barbie and Become Mrs. Potato Head?
Copyright © 2003 by Mary Pierce

Requests for information should be addressed to:
Zondervan, *Grand Rapids, Michigan 49530*

Library of Congress Cataloging-in-Publication Data

Pierce, Mary, 1949–
    When did I stop being Barbie and become Mrs. Potato Head? : learning to
    embrace the woman you've become / by Mary Pierce.
        p. cm.
    ISBN 0-310-24856-6
    1. Middle aged women. 2. Aging — Psychological aspects. 3. Aging — Reli-
    gious aspects — Christianity. 4. Aging — Humor. I. Title.
    HQ1059.4.P54   2003
    305.244 — dc21
                                                                    2003008677

Published in association with the literary agency of Alive Communications, Inc., 7680
Goddard St., Suite 200, Colorado Springs, Colorado 80920.

Interior design by Susan Ambs

Printed in the United States of America

04 05 06 07 08 09 /❖ DC/ 10 9 8 7 6 5 4

For my mother,
who taught me to laugh

Contents

ACKNOWLEDGMENTS

Thanks to all the women in my life for their inspiration, encouragement, advice, prayers, stories, tears, and laughter. Thanks especially to my mother, Lee Scholljegerdes, who taught me how to live and gave me so much material. Thanks to my mother-in-law, Beverly Pierce, who prays because "God can see around the corners!" To my daughters, Katy Berry, Lizz Berry, Laura Urbalejo, and Jenny Keys: What beautiful young women you all are, and what a privilege it is to be your mother and your friend!

To my sisters: Carol Persons, Jeanette Wuollett, Janie Wuollett, Maureen Conroy, Sue, Karen, and Patty Pierce, Cary Kaufman Gershon and her mom, Esther (my "other mother"), Joanne Malloy, Kathy Wile, Lindy Gardner, Nancy Moulton, Karen Biel, Lil Larson, and Charlene Vlcek—thank you all for your sisterly love. (And thank you, Karen West Hebert, for the clarinet!)

Thanks to the women who kept me going: Linda Glasford, my first agent at Alive Communications, Allison Gappa Bottke (for believing in me and for connecting me with Alive), and my writing coach Joan Webb. (Joan, you were right. I did not die in the quicksand!)

Thanks to my writing friends, like Joyce Ellis, in the Minnesota and Western Wisconsin Christian Writers' Guilds, and my critiquing friends, Beth Ellie, Joann Olson, Karen Olson, Becky Deinger, and Sheila Wilkinson, for saving me from embarrassment. Thanks to (*très* helpful) Kelly Conroy for saving me from embarrassing myself in languages other than English.

Thanks to my editor, Sandy Vander Zicht, who made it all happen, for her insightful suggestions and great feel for this material.

Thanks to my friends at Focus on the Family—thanks to former editor Bonnie Shepherd for the launch, and to editor Susan Graham and the rest of the team for making the flight so enjoyable. What a privilege it's been to work with all of you!

There are men to thank as well: to my sons Alex Berry (thanks for asking, "If you don't write your stories, who will?") and Danny Pierce. (Well done, boys!) Thanks to my brothers David and Jeff Wuollett, Tom, Mark, and Todd Pierce and Dan Conroy for your laughter and encouragement. Thanks to Rod Larson and Mark Halvorsen at WWIB radio for inviting me on the air, to web wizard Chris Jeub at Focus for connecting me, and to Lee Hough, my agent at Alive, for believing we have a future together.

And thanks most deeply to my husband, Terry. Patient partner and faithful friend, you are God's surprising and delightful gift to me and to our family. Thank you, Terry, for saving my life.

Thank you, God, for second chances.

AUTHOR'S NOTE

Dear Reader,

I love reading books that offer me answers. Even more, I love reading books that raise questions and give me something to think about. Sometimes a question will become a starting point for personal journaling. Sometimes a question will launch discussions with others.

At the end of each chapter, you'll find some questions—some points to ponder—to do with as you wish. Perhaps you'll use them for your own reflection or journaling. Perhaps they'll open up areas of discussion with your family or friends. Perhaps you'll use them with a book discussion group. Whatever you choose to do, have fun!

Joy to you today,

Mary Pierce

INTRODUCTION

If you're thinking, *I've never been a fashion doll like Barbie!*— let me assure you, neither have I. Not for a second! In the last fifty-plus years I have been (not necessarily in this order): daughter, sister, wife, mother, daughter-in-law, sister-in-law, student, saxophone player, sales clerk, secretary, waitress, administrative assistant, belly dancer, second wife (I don't *think* those last two had anything to do with each other), stepmother, mother-in-law, grandmother, piano player, teacher, typist, student again in midlife, supervisor, trainer, stockbroker, writer, and speaker. (I obviously can't hold a job . . .)

I don't believe in reincarnation; once around this life is more than enough for me! But I do believe in *reconfiguration,* and God has certainly "reconfigured" me more than once. Perhaps he's done the same for you. You probably have a list similar to mine, longer or shorter depending on how long you've been adding to your resumé. "Fashion doll" isn't on my list, and it probably isn't on yours either, but that hasn't stopped us from dreaming, has it?

I've dreamed that one day, if I just lost that ten (okay, thirty!) pounds, if I just learned to love jogging, if I just took up Tae Bo . . . then one day, I would look like that ideal female image. Sleek. Fit. Gorgeous.

That dream of perfection has, alas, eluded me my entire life. In my twenties, it was the bean dip and tortilla chips working against me. In my thirties, I blamed the "baby fat" lingering longer and lower from each of my three pregnancies. In my forties, gravity began to have its way with me and my metabolism went into reverse. Now, in my fifties, here I sit—slouch, actually—contemplating the sorry state of my body, face, and hair, wondering, *Will I ever measure up to the ideal? Will I ever get myself totally "together"?*

The answer to those questions is: Not in this lifetime. Not in a thousand lifetimes!

Why not? Because the "together" of my dreams is humanly impossible to achieve. Let me repeat that. Humanly impossible. The idea of this "ideal" woman is out of whack. Not achievable. Can't be done. Impossible.

I-M-P-O-S-S-I-B-L-E.

Still, I dream . . .

I've told you a little about me. Who are you?

Maybe you *have* always felt like a fashion doll, and you are reading this book so you can find out how the rest of us live. You have some kind of morbid curiosity, like those people who slow down next to a car crash on the freeway. You're reading this so you can congratulate yourself, "At least I'm not a mess like she is!" Welcome to you.

Maybe, like me, you've always felt a little too big in some places, a little too flat in others, a little too slow, a little too saggy, a little too out of shape, a little too tired—or sometimes all of the above at once. Welcome to you, too, and take heart. Some of those girls who used to feel like fashion dolls have caught up with us. We could say we were just ahead of our time.

Whoever you are, whatever your reasons for reading this, welcome! This is a book about women. All kinds of women. I hope you'll find some laughter and maybe some new things to think about.

I hope on these pages you'll see someone you recognize.

She might even be you.

Come and listen, all you who fear God;
let me tell you what he has done for me.

Psalm 66:16

How It All Began

CHAPTER ONE

"Act your shoe size! Be a child again! Play more!" The motivational speaker shouted his prescription for stress relief. *Act my shoe size? How,* I wondered, *does an eight-and-a-half-year-old act?* Could I even remember?

My friend Karen started acting her shoe size when she turned fifty. She began collecting Barbie dolls. "Why Barbie?" I asked as I examined the 1963 Fashion Queen Barbie she had just scored on eBay. This doll came complete with a white-and-gold-lamé striped swimsuit, a matching turban, and three wigs—blonde, brunette, and red.

"I don't remember any red-haired Barbies," I said.

"That's not red. It's titian," Karen corrected me.

"Pardon me," I said. I had no fashion sense whatsoever. "Tell me again. Why Barbie?"

"We were so poor when I was little, I only had one doll—a Barbie doll," Karen explained. "She got lost in the shuffle when we moved, and I've always wanted another. I'm in my second childhood, I guess."

17

It's a nice bonus in life when we get to live out our childhood longings—like eating a whole box of Twinkies by yourself. Or a whole gallon of ice cream. Or a whole pound of bacon. (You understand now why I never identified much with Barbie.)

Collecting Barbie and her accessories was great for my friend Karen who grew up in Southern California and has managed to maintain her face and her slim, fit figure. Like the fashion dolls, she dresses in coordinated outfits with more than a little pizzazz. She's from "the coast," and like all women from either coast, she has "that certain something"—sparkle, élan, a Big City air about her.

I, on the other hand, am from the Midwest, and—the obvious cultural panache of the Chicago stockyards aside—girls from my part of the country tend to be considered, well, sturdy. Not terribly glamorous. We're the ones whose grandfathers bragged that their women were "strong, like bulls." We're the ones whose favorite color is brown, as long as it's not too exciting a shade of brown.

It was quite an aesthetic shock for us when Barbie came along. Va-va-va-voom! Barbie had the hair, the legs—and let's be honest, the breasts—of our dreams. She had the clothes, the house, and the cars of our fantasies. Hers was the life we wanted. She even had our dream man.

We longed for our own Ken, a dreamboat who would love us without reservation, always be near us, and always be ready for our next adventure together. The perfect man for our happily ever after.

I'm evidently still dreaming some of those dreams, all these years later. Why else would I have tried every fad diet that's hit the market? Why else would I have three wardrobes, in three different sizes, in my closet? Why else would I have this vague sense, almost all my life, of not being quite good enough, not pretty enough, not cool enough, not measuring up to the ideal? Why else, when I look in the mirror at my perfectly acceptable five-foot-seven-inch frame, do I still imagine what it would be like to be five-foot-ten, weigh 110 pounds, and have size-three feet? It's got to be Barbie. She's haunting me.

EMBRACING MY INNER GIRL

A few days after visiting my real-life Barbie friend Karen, I was driving around doing my grown-up errands, and I got to thinking about what that motivational speaker said. What did it mean to "act your shoe size"?

"Okay, Inner Eight-and-a-Half-Year-Old," I said aloud in the car. "What do you want to do?" The answer came instantly, as if I had a backseat full of kids screaming, "We want toys! We want toys!"

"All right, all right!" I said as I headed for Target. "But you're only getting one! And if you start misbehaving in the store, we're going straight home." I glanced in the rearview mirror and remembered I was alone. My inner girl giggled.

"Don't make me stop this car," I muttered.

In Target, I stood for a moment in the toy department, taking deep breaths. I didn't feel like a harried mother, as I had on so many past Christmas trips to this department. I felt nothing like a doting grandmother, as I had on more recent occasions. I just stood in the aisle, looking down the long rows of primary-colored delight, taking it all in.

I felt small, almost like the child I used to be. I was tempted to get down on my knees to gain a true child's perspective, but was embarrassed by the thought of having to call store security to help me back up. And I was afraid bending like that might cause permanent damage to my knees.

I strolled through the toy department, looking at the dizzying display of merchandise, listening for something to speak to my inner girl. I passed an array of army men, G.I. Joe and his buddies; they were all my brothers' shoe sizes. The assorted toy cars and trucks in all makes and models didn't appeal to me either. They reminded me of adult problems like repair bills and midnight calls to unlock the kids' cars. (Why do such calls always come at midnight, during a blizzard?)

My inner child tugged at my pant leg, urging me to the next aisle. I turned the corner. The doll aisle. *Oh goody,* my inner girl said. *This is more like it.*

DOLL FREAK

I had been an eight-year-old doll freak. I had a Tiny Tears baby doll (cousin to Betsy Wetsy) that came with miniature Ivory soap, Johnson's baby powder, and her own wee little washcloth and miniature towel. A tiny plastic baby bottle was included, and she wore a diaper. She was actually a future mommy training tool, disguised as a doll, but we were clueless. "Drinks, wets, and cries real tears," was this baby doll's selling point. The same could be said for her today, if she were repackaged as "Menopause Doll." I'd buy one, just for the companionship.

Back then I also had a huge (by little girl standards) stuffed rag doll named Lulu. One day, a neighbor boy whacked Lulu across my brother's knee and her head flew off. My mother sewed it back on. Several times. Lulu taught me one of the enduring lessons of womanhood: When life whacks you so hard your head flies off, sew it back on and keep going. After a while, Lulu had lost so much of her stuffing she could no longer remain upright without support. I know that feeling.

A rubber-skinned doll I called Linda had cotton stuffing that had gotten wet and then moldy. She stunk, but I couldn't get rid of her. My friend Cary and I played "doll wedding" in our living room and, since Ken and G.I. Joe hadn't been invented yet, we made Linda the groom. Linda's foul odor didn't seem so out of character when she was pretending to be a boy.

For Christmas the year I was in sixth grade, my mother gave me a bride doll. She was dressed in a beautiful white gown and veil. Supposedly an adult female, this bride was flat-chested, with chubby child legs and Mary Jane shoes. She may have been dressed like a grown-up bride, but, underneath it all, she was just a little girl. (Aren't all young brides?) She was my last doll.

I got kind of misty, standing there in Target remembering all those happy hours. Then I spotted the Barbie dolls. I sighed. My inner girl sighed. My friend Karen and her inner seven-year-old loved Barbie, but was Barbie for us? Had she ever been? I'd never been that glamorous, and certainly never that top-heavy. I didn't need a fashion doll reminding me how far I was from the ideal.

I gave up trying to find the right doll. My inner girl was disappointed; she needed the consolation of a hot fudge sundae. We headed out of the toy department when, suddenly, I saw her—the doll that sang out to my heart, speaking not only to the child I once was but to the woman I am today.

MRS. POTATO HEAD

I picked up the box and the memories flooded my mind— fond memories of real potatoes poked full of plastic eyes and lips, ears and arms. Real potatoes lying under the bed for days, shriveling and rotting, until my mother went snooping to find the source of the stench.

"What is this?" she'd shriek, holding the wrinkled mess up for inspection.

"Grandma Potato Head?" I'd suggest.

Mrs. Potato Head had been a favorite toy back then, and I knew in an instant that she represented my true self, then and today. The real me was not a sweet innocent baby doll and certainly not a sleek, sophisticated fashion doll. Mrs. Potato Head was the very image of the sturdy, sensible girl I'd always been and the sturdy, sensible woman I'd become. This was the toy that made my inner child want to skip all the way home.

Later at home at my kitchen table, I assembled Mrs. Potato Head carefully, following the illustrations on the box. I realized immediately that Mrs. Potato Head is a middle-aged woman.

She's low fat, high fiber, and high carb—all of which I strive to be. She comes with reading glasses and a sun visor. She knows the UV ray is not her friend.

Into the holes in Mrs. P's plastic body, I inserted her eyes (my favorite shade of periwinkle), her round nose, and her full red lips. Mrs. Potato Head had evidently read the same beauty advice articles I'd read; she knew that lipstick is a necessity for women over forty. She also knew that the most important thing to remember when putting on lipstick is to agree with God about where your lips should end.

I inserted her ears and added her loop earrings, slipped her arms into place just under her ears, and then stuck on her feet. I stood her on the table. I noticed her middle-age spread had sunk so low she no longer had knees. Oh, yeah. My kind of woman.

I hung her red plastic purse on her arm and sat back to admire my handiwork. My heart sang. Yes! Mrs. Potato Head evoked images from my childhood—endearing, sweet images. She made me smile, relieved my stress. I felt eight-and-a-half again, and it was grand.

Later that day, I came through the kitchen and glanced at Mrs. Potato Head. One of my daughters had obviously seen her too, for Mrs. P's full red lips had been removed, and in their place, she was sticking out her pink plastic tongue. A *'tater with attitude,* I thought. She made me smile again.

Later that same day, I walked by and noticed Mrs. P's sun visor was missing, leaving her head shining and bald. One of her earrings was hanging from her tongue. Shaving her head and piercing her tongue was a bold fashion move for a middle-aged woman. *Go for it, Mrs. P*, I thought. *Just go for it!*

Mrs. Potato Head is a lot like me—perfectly ordinary. Like me, she's a little lumpy and a little dumpy compared to the high-fashion dolls and the high-tech toys, but she's capable of "copping an attitude" when necessary.

I moved Mrs. Potato Head to my office, where she looks down at me as I write, reminding me every day that laughter is as necessary to good health as water and air, fiber and vitamins. Ten laughs is my minimum daily requirement. To get that, it helps if I act my shoe size once in a while.

> *A cheerful disposition is good for your health;*
> *gloom and doom leave you bone-tired.*
>
> > *Proverbs 17:22 The Message*

POINTS TO PONDER

1. What's your shoe size? What would you do if you "acted your shoe size"?

2. Describe your favorite toy from childhood. What warm memories does it bring? What would it be like to have that toy today?

3. If you had the original toy in its original packaging would you:
   (a) Offer it to the highest bidder on eBay? *(It must be worth a fortune by now!)*
   (b) Keep it locked in a glass case on display? *(Look but don't touch!)*
   (c) Let your children or grandchildren play with it? *(It's only a toy, for heaven's sake!)*

   Defend your position.

What's Funny Today, Lord?

CHAPTER TWO

Laughter—that daily requirement for good mental health—is a gift from God. It's healing, and it makes us feel younger. That's why I decided to start each day asking, "What's funny today, Lord?" Ask and ye shall receive.

I'm not a morning person. I can roll out of bed, take my shower, and be half-dressed before I even begin to wake up. One morning I stepped out of the shower, grabbed the hair mousse, filled my palms with the fluffy goop, and, still half asleep, slapped it on my cheeks. It dried in seconds, giving me an instant face-lift—much cheaper than plastic surgery.

God's greatest kindness, I've heard, is that the eyes go as the wrinkles come. I have one of those magnifying makeup mirrors on the counter in my bathroom. The mirror has a strip of lights—*très* Hollywood—on each side. I'm certain a young person with perfect skin invented this mirror. Nobody over forty wants to see their face so up close and personal, in light bright enough to perform microsurgery, illuminating every wrinkle, dent, and sag.

I don't like the mirror, but with the lights and the magnification, I can put on my makeup without wearing my bifocals or contacts. The mirror has several lighting options. The "daylight" setting is the cruelest; nothing is hidden under the sun. "Office" imitates the irritating glare of fluorescent lighting for those who want to recreate workplace pallor at home. Set on "evening," the soft lights give my skin a lovely radiance. But what good does it do? A girl can't very well haul the mirror with her for a night on the town, turn it on at the table, and ask her dinner date, "Would you please hold this over my face while I eat my lobster? I want to glow."

Some days I think a "midnight" setting might be nice. The darkness would be a welcome relief—no wrinkles, no age spots, no sagging. The only concern would be jamming my mascara wand into my eyeball, but I do that in "daylight" now anyway.

Looking at my magnified face one morning, I asked aloud, "What's funny today, Lord?" I smiled into the mirror. Maybe it was the distortion of the magnifying side or the glare of the lights, but I looked like Jack Nicholson—in his role as the Joker in *Batman*.

I ran to my husband, who was minding his own business watching the morning news in the adjacent bedroom.

"Honey," I cried, "do you think I look like Jack Nicholson?"

He didn't even look up. "In which movie?" he asked.

Très amusing.

GOOD MEDICINE

Laughter lifts our spirits and may even be heart healthy, according to medical studies. One expert said such research confirms the old axiom that "laughter is the best medicine." Those experts could have saved a lot of time, to say nothing of thousands of research dollars, if they had just read Proverbs 17:22, where that "old axiom" comes from: "A joyful heart is good medicine" (NASB). It's nice when modern science confirms what God told us ages ago.

We can stay heart healthy, according to the experts, by finding humor in day-to-day situations. They gave an example of such humor: "You arrive at a party and discover someone else is wearing your same outfit. How do you respond?"

I can tell you how I responded when I arrived at a fancy business function one night. I had dressed with care in my best outfit—a black velveteen jacket with a white ruffly blouse and my best black slacks. To my horror, I saw that the entire catering staff was dressed exactly like me. Call me a sourpuss, but I didn't find this one bit funny.

During the evening, one of the caterers handed me a tray of crab puffs. I took one and said, "Thanks." He glared at me, pushed the tray toward me, and hissed, "Start passing!"

I decided I had nothing to lose. I met several interesting gentlemen as I passed the canapés. One asked me for directions to the men's room. One asked me to get his coat from the checkroom. A third asked me if I could retrieve his Mercedes from valet parking. A fourth offered me a tip. I was tempted.

"Someday you'll laugh about this," I told myself as I drove home that night. Several decades later, I can laugh about it, but I still cringe at the sight of hors d'œuvres.

Our laughing muscles, science tells us, become stronger with exercise. But a titter or a chuckle, just saying "ha ha," is like doing an occasional sit-up. What we need are more good, hearty laughs, but how? Since so much of humor is related to surprise, to the unexpected—how do we engineer opportunities for belly laughs?

Try installing more mirrors in the house. Nothing tickles the funny bone like the sight of you taking yourself too seriously. I should have had a mirror near the kitchen table the day I stood there lecturing my seven-year-old son. I talked at length while he stared up at me, riveted. I was certain that, even at his tender age, he appreciated my wisdom. After several minutes, I asked him, "Do you understand what Mother means?"

"Huh?" he said. Then he asked earnestly, "Did you know that when you talk the hair in your nose wiggles?"

Installing a full-length mirror in my bathroom (what was I thinking?) has given me lots of laughs, between the tears. Seeing my back for the first time in ages, I realized I'd developed "back fat." I'd already been battling the bulge of my thighs and my derriere. I'd already bemoaned my widening hips, sagging stomach, and the ever-flappier chicken wings on the backs of my upper arms. But back fat? What was this new treachery?

There it was, bulging above and below my bra. I could tell by looking at it that it would be tough to deal with. I was tempted to call the local Sports R Us Club, but I could just imagine what would happen . . .

A girl named Krissy answers the phone at the health club. She sounds about ten. I ask, "Do you have a machine to get rid of back fat?"

"Ewww! What's that?"

I explain my problem. She says, "That is totally disgusting. Oops. Did I say that out loud?"

"It's okay," I say, but it's not really. It's okay if *I'm* disgusted. It's *my* back fat, after all. Krissy is supposed to be a health care professional. But then again, she is only ten.

"Just a minute," Krissy says. "I'll get Troy. He's the weekend manager." *Troy? He's probably twelve.*

I explain my problem to him. To his credit, Troy doesn't say "ewww" once. But I hear him stifling a chuckle, covering the mouthpiece as he shushes Krissy. When Troy finally speaks, it's in careful, measured tones, though his voice keeps breaking. Is it laughter or puberty? I can't be sure.

"The only solution for back fat is the Push Away," he says.

At last, we're making some progress! I envision some high-tech, high-tension, fat-blasting, strength-building, body-shaping miracle of modern equipment design. "What's a Push Away?" I ask.

Troy pauses ever so slightly. I hear Krissy snorting in the background. "That's where you 'push away' from the dinner table. That'll take care of your back fat!" Troy is snorting now, too, and his voice gets higher and higher. Finally, breathlessly, he squeaks, "It also works for chicken wings." He hangs up.

I wonder if they have Prince Albert in the can at Sports R Us. I'd better call on Monday, when the grown-up manager is in.

THE BIG PICTURE

Ask God to show you what's funny and he will. He invented laughter and designed us to benefit from it. He made it good medicine. Laugh heartily and often. Develop a low joy threshold. Did you know that just a few seconds of smiling will fool your brain into thinking you're actually happy? (Try it. Right now. No one is watching. Go ahead. Smile.)

While you're smiling, remember the big picture. The key to lasting contentment God also invented. While we're living this life, coping with changes, the key is to "fix our eyes not on what is seen, but on what is unseen. For what is seen is temporary, but what is unseen is eternal" (2 Corinthians 4:18).

This truth was illustrated perfectly by two women I overheard in a restaurant the other day. As they ate lunch together, one woman lamented, "I just hate getting older. Every day I look in the mirror and see a new wrinkle!"

Her wise friend replied, "So? Stop looking in the mirror."

What great advice. And so simple. Stop looking in the mirror.

The less I look in the mirror, the more I'll notice other people. The less attention I pay to my wrinkles or my aches and pains, the more attention I'll pay to what really matters in the grand scheme of things. Who can I encourage with a phone call or a note? Who needs a laugh? Who needs comfort? Who needs prayer? With whom can I share my blessings—my time, my money, and my energy?

In God's grand scheme, our troubles here are only temporary. I can appreciate the truth of this good news: "Therefore we do not lose heart. Though outwardly we are wasting away, yet inwardly we are being renewed day by day" (2 Corinthians 4:16).

Renewed daily by God's generosity. Renewed daily by laughter. Renewed daily with an anointing of the "oil of joy" (Hebrews 1:9). And a joyful heart—that is, a heart full of the joy of knowing God—is, indeed, the best medicine for whatever is ailing us.

> *When anxiety was great within me,*
> *your consolation brought joy to my soul.*
>
> *Psalm 94:19*

POINTS TO PONDER

1. Describe your most embarrassing moment. Did you laugh about it then? Can you now?

2. For three days, keep track of things that make you laugh. Note if the incident brought you a smile, a chuckle, or a belly laugh. After three days, analyze your laugh habits. What did you discover about your sense of humor?

3. List five things you've always thought would be fun to try. Why haven't you tried them? What's stopping you now?

Fit to Be Tied

One Monday morning, shortly after I discovered my back fat, I did call the Sports R Us Athletic Club. I talked to the grown-up manager, and before I knew it, I'd signed up for a three-month trial membership and a dance-fitness class. I hesitated before signing up. I knew an athletic club wasn't for me. The very name implied something I wasn't. But a dance class? What could be so hard about that? I loved dancing.

I worried a little that the class would be full of tight and toned women who had been dancing their way to fitness for years—women who had never had to wrestle an extra Butterball or two off their waist. Walking into the first class laid those fears to rest. These were women just like me.

A long T-shirt over sweats, which hides a multitude of brownie sundaes, was standard apparel. I sensed a spirit of fun. I could enjoy this. These were just nice women wanting to firm up a little. Or so I thought.

Then the music started. Krissy was our teacher. She wasn't ten after all. She was a dynamic little spitfire, about twenty-two, and absolutely perfect.

"Are you READY?" Krissy shrieked into her headset. Her voice reverberated off the walls.

"Yeah!" the class yelled back, and the music started pounding.

"Let's GO-O-O-O!" Krissy screamed. "And it's STEP and LIFT and STRETCH and KICK and JUMP and SWAY and TOUCH and TUCK! ABS, ladies! Hold in those ABS!"

Abs? What abs? I hadn't thought about mine for over two decades, since the last time I'd given birth. "Lift! Kick! Stretch!" Krissy hollered.

I was lost in a minute-and-a-half. The class had obviously heard all this before and had practiced at home. I stretched when I should have squeezed, lunged when I should have tucked. The class moved right, I went left. They moved forward, and I was run over by the woman behind me. I was inept. A complete klutz.

In this moment of abject hopelessness, I noticed a woman about my age, two rows ahead of me on my right. She wore a body-hugging leotard, not that she had much body to hug. Her calves were sculpted granite above her aerobically correct footwear. Her headband was color-coordinated to her outfit. Even her hair looked fit. She lunged and lifted, tucked and squeezed on cue. And she added little hops everywhere for extra aerobic benefit. "Hopper" was trim and cute. And she was giving me a headache.

To save my flagging sense of self-worth, I focused on the woman to my left. She was uncoordinated and out of shape. Her muscles looked like they'd been on sabbatical for years.

In horror, I realized I was next to the mirrored wall. I smiled weakly at my reflection. *Hang in there. You'll survive. You've had children.*

Krissy told us to pick up our weights. *Impossible!* I thought, and then realized she meant our handheld weights. Hopper reached into her gym bag and whipped out weights color-matched to her outfit. They were the size of small dogs. My little one-pounders looked more like hot dogs.

Krissy shouted encouragement. "Think bicep! Tricep! Deltoid! Trapezius!"

I turned to the gal behind me. "Do I have those?" I asked.

"You'll know tomorrow," she said. I believed her.

"And it's up-two-three-hold. And down-two-three-relax. And it's up . . ." I hefted. I held. I relaxed. *I'm doing it! I'm lifting. Hey, this is easy. What are those body builders always sweating about?* My muscles chose that moment to protest. I felt tension, then quivering, and then complete surrender. I heard them chanting, "No! No! We won't go!"

Come on, girls, I begged silently. *Just a couple more repetitions.* They responded with, "Two-four-six-eight! We won't lift another weight!" and tuned me out. I knew they were thinking about a hot bath and a liniment rub.

I stopped and watched Hopper pumping away, sweating nary a drop. Her chiseled biceps flexed with military precision, and her triceps bore no trace of those chicken wings that wave at me in the mirror every morning as I do my hair. Hopper even put a little extra hop into her lifts. I hated her.

What am I doing here? I thought. *My grandma never took a class like this . . .*

GRANDMA'S GLAMOUR STRETCHER

Grandma got all the exercise she needed doing housework for her family of twelve. She competed weekly in the Laundry Olympics—the Monday-Wash-Day-Tuesday-Ironing-Day Biathlon. She pumped water, boiled it, and scrubbed clothes on the washboard. She bent and stretched again and again hanging clothes on the line—fifty-two weeks a year, summer and winter, in Minnesota. Bend and stretch, tug and lift, hold and release. Repeat. Again. And again.

In the winter, she got plenty of exercise chopping wood and firing up the stove to thaw Grandpa's frozen long johns. In the spring, she got a nice aerobic benefit chasing the neighbor's dog down the road after he ran through the clothes on the line and got her unmentionables wrapped around his neck.

When she was in her eighties, Grandma moved into a little house in the country, right next door to my aunt and uncle. The small, easily managed house offered a restful retirement. Maybe she missed the housework, or maybe she missed Grandpa, but in that house, Grandma discovered Jack LaLanne, television's exercise guru of the 1960s, the father of the fitness movement.

Each morning, she faithfully followed LaLanne's instructions, working out in her little house, performing her calisthenics, stretches, and bends. She appreciated how Jack called out encouragement to the viewing audience.

"Come on, Mrs. Larson! You can do it," he'd say, or "That's it, Helga. Keep going!" Grandma didn't know any Helga, but she knew several Mrs. Larsons. And so, evidently, did Jack.

Grandma ordered a Jack LaLanne "Glamour Stretcher," which was a thick rubber cord with a handle on each end. Holding the handles and spreading her arms wide to stretch the band, Grandma worked her biceps, triceps, delts, and pecs, without even realizing it.

One summer morning, when I was thirteen, I was visiting my aunt and uncle and my cousin Duane, who was fourteen. Duane and I watched from their front window as Grandma stood on the lawn next door with her Glamour Stretcher.

The morning sun sparkled through the trees as Grandma opened her arms wide, stretching that rubber cord as far as her arms would reach. Through the open window, we heard her counting off in Finnish.

We watched Grandma in silence, and then Duane started chanting, in time to her movements, a familiar joke line: "We must, we must, we must increase our bust . . ." I was mortified by this reference to the female anatomy—especially Grandma's anatomy. I slugged him. He laughed and left the room.

I watched my grandmother as she continued her regimen, listened to her lilting accent as she switched from counting to singing a song from her past. She stretched on and on. She smiled, ageless out there, enjoying the movement, the music, and the moment. She was beautiful.

COUNTING CALORIES

I remember Grandma and wonder if we've taken the fitness craze a little too far. I've seen several books lately on the subject of "wedding fitness." As if a bride doesn't have enough to do without worrying about her deltoids. As if knowing that a slice of wedding cake contains three thousand calories is going to stop her from eating it. As if Mr. Right proposed with, "Will you be my wife . . . but only if you get in shape first?" Bridal bicep building? How strong do you have to be to hold the bouquet, or even to toss it? Wedding workouts? Good grief! It's an aisle, not the Boston Marathon.

What we need are marriage fitness books, books that could prepare us for the energy demands of life after "the two become one." Where are the calorie charts for real life?

Calories required to move his dirty socks from the floor to the hamper six inches away (15). Calories burned in angry outburst when his dirty socks are found on top of the hamper (200). Calories expended cleaning the house (500). Calories used recleaning the house after you turn around and see that your toddler has been "helping" you as you've been cleaning (2000). Calories consumed giving birth (5000). Calories burned worrying for the next twenty-two years (uncountable).

Who needs a gym membership? Lifting babies, hauling groceries, dozens of trips up and down the stairs, doing the laundry, cleaning up after everyone, running around like crazy, walking the floor at night—it all counts. Take the credit. Your grandmother would have.

OH, TO BE CONTENT . . .

Back at Sports R Us, Krissy ended the dance-fitness session with a cooldown. I needed it. My furnace was running hot. I'd probably burned an extra five pounds of fat just envying Hopper. *I could look like that too, if I had hours and hours every week to indulge in self-preservation. She probably has nothing better to do than primp and preen . . .*

I was wrong. Hopper, I found out after class, had five kids. I heard this from a classmate who assured me Hopper was a very nice person. "She sings opera, runs marathons, and delivers meals to the homebound in her spare time."

How perfect can one woman be? I groaned. I noticed my shoe was untied. As I bent over to tie it, I banged my head against the stack of aerobic steps. I considered not coming back up.

While I was down there, I got to thinking. What was this all about? Was this a quest for physical perfection? If so, it was futile. Physical perfection is impossible in this world. What if the dance class and other exercise provided Hopper with the energy she needed for her busy life? What if her goal was to be fit so she could enjoy her life, not to let being fit *become* her life? Maybe fitness was the means to an end, not an end in itself.

I realized I was the one obsessing about all this, not Hopper. She was coming here, getting a workout, and moving on to more important things. Perhaps I could do that, too. I decided to start taking better care of myself, so I could live my life.

I've been clumsy and I've been coordinated. I've been fatter and I've been slimmer. I can learn to be content in all circumstances by doing the most important exercise of all: getting on my knees and submitting my will to God.

Thinking it over, I'll be exercising my prerogative to take better care of myself, and to have some fun with this whole fitness thing. To worry less about this body, which is wasting away, and focus my attention on the things that matter.

I want to be ready when God calls me to his aerobic routine, the one that's truly good for the heart. Ready to get down on my knees more often, and pray more fervently. Ready—and able—to get back up, and take leaps of faith as I follow his plan for my future. Ready to reach out beyond my comfort zone to those in need, and be strong enough to help them, strong enough to hang on for the long term.

I want to be strong. I want to be ready. Ready for God. Ready for life.

> *There are different kinds of service, but the same Lord. There are different kinds of working, but the same God works all of them in all men.*
>
> *1 Corinthians 12:5–6*

POINTS TO PONDER

1. Describe your own "fitness journey." What have you tried? Where are you now?

2. Thinking about your physical body, complete this sentence: "I wish my _____ could be _____ and my ____ could be _____." What difference would these changes make?

3. Describe your ideal physical self (weight, fitness level, etc.) as if she already existed. (For example, "I weigh [ideal] pounds. I exercise . . .") What is one step you can take this week in that direction?

The Eyes Have Had It!

CHAPTER FOUR

Sophie Tucker supposedly said, "From her birth to her teens, a girl needs good parents. From eighteen to thirty-five, she needs good looks. From thirty-five to fifty, she needs a good personality. From fifty on, a girl needs cash."

She also needs glasses. I bought my first pair of reading glasses the day I turned forty, the day my grasp of the words in my *Wall Street Journal* fell short of my reach. Running to the drugstore across the street from my office, I found the rack of reading glasses hidden in the back of the store, near the pharmacy counter. They do this on purpose, so that the newly middle-aged, already self-conscious about their need for readers, can pretend to be browsing for vitamins, muscle-building protein powder, or birth-control products, instead of buying reading glasses—a product that screams, "Hey! I'm getting old!"

After an hour's deliberation, I selected a pair of black-framed glasses that, in the warped little mirror at the top of the rack, made me look like a seriously intellectual Sophia Loren. I later realized, looking in a real mirror at home, that if I added a black plastic mustache to the glasses, I could pass for Groucho Marx.

On the way to the checkout counter, I grabbed a bottle of Oil of Somebody's Super Anti-Wrinkle Formula and a tube of Ben Gay. I was ready for middle age. Happy birthday to me.

For almost a decade, I battled the drugstore reading glasses war, on a crusade to find the perfect readers, the perfect blend of fashion and function. I bought different colors, coordinating them with my work outfits. I went through a navy blue phase, a red stage, and a purple period. I tried wire-rimmed, round lenses. I looked like John Lennon. I chose giant lenses. I looked like The Fly. I bought one pair with thick frames that made them easy to find on the nightstand in the dark—handy for night raids on the refrigerator. Their weight left marks on my nose and gave me a headache, and they made me gain ten pounds.

On and on the battle raged. I raided rack after rack of cheap glasses as it became harder and harder to read. I finally surrendered and made a visit to a "real" eye doctor, one that sold "real" glasses.

Diagnosis: "You can't read. In fact, you can't see."

"Tell me something I don't know," I said.

"You're officially middle-aged," he said. "Congratulations. You need bifocals." *Ouch.*

What an amazing difference my new bifocals made as I drove home. I could see birds and flowers, children playing, neighbors waving. Our house.

"The trees have leaves again!" I told my husband that evening. "And did you know those little green signs at the intersections actually tell you what street you're on?"

He made a little strangling noise and sputtered, "You mean . . . you mean you've been driving all this time, and . . ."

I cut him off midsentence. "Hey, I could see pretty well when I squinted. Usually."

"Remind me to do all the driving from now on," he said as he headed for the garage to check the car for dents. Oh, he of little faith.

Bifocals suited me fine, once I learned how to hold my head right so the stairs didn't disappear as I was descending. No more hassling with lost glasses. I was content—content, that is, until the day I saw an ad for a new invention: bifocal contacts.

I had never been a contact wearer, but these promised me the best of both worlds—a close-up reading world, and the faraway big picture at the same time. Best of all, they gave the illusion of not needing glasses at all. This was a veritable fountain of youth! I ran to my eye doctor and got fitted with the soft plastic lenses with concentric circles.

"The circles provide, alternately, distance vision and close-up vision," the doctor explained. "Your eyes will learn to 'select' the correct circles in a few days."

We spent the next few days on vacation at Disney World, where my eyes refused to select the correct circles. My new contacts distorted everything into fun house mirror images—fat to skinny to fat, tall to short to tall again. I saw gigantic rodents at every corner. Minuscule toddlers scurried about my feet. The theme from "It's a Small World" mocked me. It was a small world, after all. No, wait! It was a big world. Small! Big! Small! Big! Around and around I went.

"Want to go on the roller coaster?" my husband asked.

"You mean I'm *not?*" I wailed. I hurried back to the hotel room and removed the contacts. Slipping my glasses on in relief, I resolved that bifocals would be newfangled enough for me. I was content. For a whole month. That's when the eye doctor suggested I try "regular" soft contacts. I agreed. I don't know why. I just did.

"You'll still have to wear reading glasses sometimes," the doctor said. I had come full circle.

The new contacts worked great, but like the doctor said, I still needed reading glasses. Many pairs of reading glasses. As the vision goes, so goes the memory. I could never remember where I left my reading glasses, so I placed several pairs strategically around the house: one in the bathroom reading basket, another near the cookbooks in the kitchen, a third at the mail sorting basket, and a fourth Velcroed to the television remote.

With all my strategic planning, how was it that there was never a pair of glasses where I needed one? Like Erma Bombeck's mysterious disappearing socks on laundry day, reading glasses disappeared into that same household black hole.

I finally bought a cord to attach to my glasses, so I could hang them around my neck. The beaded cord looked great in the store. I was sure I'd seen a picture of Sophia Loren with a cord just like it on her glasses. I hung my glasses from the cord. Sophia Loren I wasn't. Miss Murdock, my fourth grade teacher, I was.

THE GHOST OF ROCKY STONEAXE

Miss Murdock seemed ancient; she was probably in her forties. Her strict, no-nonsense teaching style and her passion for rocks and Eskimo history had earned her the nickname "Rocky Stoneaxe." To this day, I can't look at an agate without thinking of her. And anytime the Travel Channel on television takes me to the Arctic, I imagine Miss Murdock there, in her mukluks, explaining the finer points of igloo construction.

Miss Murdock's classroom smelled musty—the natural effect of her years of accumulating old rocks, bones, and animal skins. One day, I climbed the ladder to our attic, opened the access panel, stuck my head up there, and had a flashback to fourth grade. I could swear I saw Miss Murdock standing there behind my own cartons of old bones.

I could see her there in the shadows, glaring at me across the top of her reading glasses. Hers were trimmed in rhinestones (or perhaps they were pieces of geode) and lashed to her neck by that beaded cord, just like mine.

I heard her voice again. "Mary, did you want to tell the whole class what you find so funny about 'blubber'?"

I shivered in old, familiar fear. No, I didn't want to tell the class, and I didn't want to have to stay after school. Not again. Not with Miss Murdock. I ducked out, slammed the attic shut, and skedaddled down the ladder.

It was one thing the day I realized I had become my mother. It was quite another to become Rocky Stoneaxe. I whipped that beaded cord off my glasses and buried it in the bottom of the bathroom trash. It just made good fashion sense.

OF SENSES AND SENSIBILITY

This whole sight thing has me noticing other little things. We go out to dinner with friends our age. The menus arrive and we become like synchronized swimmers. We all reach for our reading glasses, perch them on our noses, and begin. In unison, we glance at the menus and glance back up at each other over the tops of our lenses. Up and down, up and down. The chiropractic profession must make a fortune adjusting the necks of people like us.

Lightbulbs, I've noticed, aren't as bright as they used to be. We need at least 250 watts to read by. We visited our adult children and couldn't see anything in their house after sundown. They don't own anything stronger than a sixty-watt bulb. For us, that's a night-light.

As my sight gets worse, I've noticed, so do my other senses. I thought the other senses were supposed to get stronger to compensate for such weakness; it ain't necessarily so. My sense of taste is *not* improved when I can't see what I'm eating. I can't *feel* the thread into the eye of the needle when I can't see the hole. And I'm not able to smell any better when I can't see what I'm smelling.

The worst of it is, when I don't have my glasses on, I can't hear either. A preacher on television last week talked about the aging process. As we get older, he said, as things in this life change, we need to hold tightly to the truth. God is not surprised by these life changes. God's purposes, his nature, and his promises do not change over time. The preacher quoted Malachi 3:6: "I, the LORD, do not change." He concluded by saying,

"Focus on the immutability of God." At least I think that's what he said. I wasn't wearing my glasses at the time.

I read about a blind mountain climber who said that blindness was a nuisance, but it wasn't a reason to not do something. What would happen, I wondered, if I started to see things that way? This vision thing is a nuisance, but it's not a reason to stop trying new things, to stop living.

What if I changed my way of seeing? What if I stopped letting "I'm too old" and "it's too late" get in my way? What if I stopped letting the fear of making a fool of myself paralyze me? I might write that poetry I've always wanted to write, take up the flute, start my own business, try standup comedy, or learn to speak Chinese.

Success is not the mountaintop, but the trek up. Success is making the journey and drawing closer to God along the way.

Meanwhile, my contacts and reading glasses work just fine, for the most part. The other day, I noticed what seemed to be a newspaper clipping on the kitchen counter. Someone in the family had clipped it and left it there. I squinted at it from across the room; the large font of the headline was just barely distinguishable with my contacts.

"NECKSHIFTED?" A chiropractic seminar perhaps? I squinted harder. What was it? "NEATSHIRTED?" A dry-cleaning ad? I found a pair of reading glasses in the silverware drawer and slipped them on as I moved closer to the ad. The letters came into focus.

"NEARSIGHTED?" it asked. Ha! I crumpled it in disgust.

And later as I read my TV program listings, the show that promised to teach me all I needed to know about the green bean turned out to be, once I put on my glasses, "The Complete History of the Green Berets."

Who needs perfect vision? This whole aging thing is really about finding a new way to see. Anyway, we live by faith, and not by sight, the Bible says. Good thing.

But my eyes are fixed on you, O Sovereign LORD.

Psalm 141:8

 **POINTS TO PONDER**

1. Complete this sentence: "I knew I was getting older when . . ."

2. Who was your favorite teacher and why?

3. What keeps you from realizing your dreams? What if you suddenly had a "new way of seeing" your limitations?

God and Picasso

Picasso's women are odd-shaped, disembodied chunks of fiercely angled female. I wonder what Picasso did to make the women in his life so mad.

I look at a Picasso woman, with her head cocked sideways and no sign of a neck, unless her neck is that lump protruding from her armpit. Her lips are locked in a grimace. Is she angry or is she just middle-aged? (Or is that redundant?)

The day she posed for Pablo, she didn't start out looking like this. In fact, for three minutes after she woke up she thought she looked just fine. Then she put on her bifocals and looked in the mirror. It's no surprise that Picasso's portrait looks as it does. He painted what he saw.

Her neck, once extending smoothly from lower lip to collarbone, is sectioned in thirds—one for each chin. Her previously unfurrowed forehead is now divided horizontally and vertically by what the medical experts call "frown lines." She knows each line of this "worry grid" intimately, by its true name: Daughter

Dates Tattooed Boy. College Tuition. Son Gets Driver's License. Mammogram Overdue. In-laws Coming for a Month.

Her arms used to hang from her shoulders like a normal person's. Now one juts from her hip and the other is wrenched behind her head. It's all that arm-twisting over the years by children begging, "Puh-leeze? Just one more piece of candy? Just one more ride on the Tilt-a-Whirl? Just one more hour past curfew?"

She used to have two eyes, set properly between her temples, and bright, young, hope-filled eyes they were. Now she has one paranoid eye in the back of her head, another wary eye to see around corners, and a third always suspicious eye she claims can see exactly what teenagers are doing—anytime, anywhere—no matter how smart they think they are.

Her legs, tired of running 24/7 to meet the demands of her family, career, and home, have decided to split. They've contorted in a way that would force a lesser woman to take a rest. Not Picasso's girl. She'll keep running, even if it is around in circles.

At least the artist caught her on a decent hair day; or maybe it's just that, compared to the rest of her, the long mane of purplish snakes doesn't look too bad. One thing is certain. Picasso got her breasts right. Hers may be at her waist, at her hips, or at her knees. It's hard to tell, but breasts never stay where they started out. It's impossible to predict just where body parts are going to settle.

This isn't Cubism, I realize. This is life.

MUSEUM MUSINGS

I wandered the National Gallery of Art in Washington, D.C., through rooms full of paintings. Monet, Manet, Gauguin, Cezanne, Homer, Van Gogh—all those names from art history in college. I wished I'd paid better attention in class.

I lingered before Raphael's "Madonna and Child with Saint John the Baptist." The drawing, nearly five hundred years old, survived to stir my soul. Later, I sat for nearly an hour in a room full of Monets, envisioning the famous artist as he recorded the simple stuff of life on canvas—hazy mornings, shimmering rivers, a bridge in fog, ordinary people. In the garden scenes, I imagined the tender touches of brush to canvas, capturing the watery image of spring rain, the subtle pastels of new life, the soft beauty of hope.

Later, in the gallery's modern art section, it occurred to me that being famous doesn't always equate with "awe-inspiring." Jackson Pollock really did dribble and splash paint. Soon he had stacks of paint-splattered canvases, and the art world looked at it all and said, "Genius!" I look at it and say, "Huh? What's the big deal? I could do that!"

But could I? Would I risk it?

If you've ever tried to sketch or paint, write or compose, you know it's harder than it looks. The artists make it look easy, but "Madonna and Child" did not appear miraculously on paper one Sunday morning as Raphael sat on the piazza, sipping cappuccino and listening to cathedral bells. Paint doesn't just splatter itself on the canvas. Even Pollock had to pick up a brush. Books, poems, and stories don't write themselves in hotel rooms while their authors bask in the poolside sun. (Darn!)

We only see the end result of days, weeks, or years of work. We see the painting but not the crumpled sketches, the mistakes, or the smudges. We don't hear the groans of frustration when the paint, or the inspiration, dries up. We read the story but never see the botched outlines, the subplots that dead-ended, and the endless revisions. We don't feel the spasms of fear at opening ourselves up to criticism, the head-banging angst that precedes public exposure. *What was I thinking? I have no talent for this! I must have been crazy to think I could do this.*

It's a lot like parenting. Every child is birthed in pain and nurtured on sacrifice and frustration. Every adult emerges at the expense of a parent's youth and sanity.

Anything worth creating exacts a price from its creator.

A LESSON IN PERSPECTIVE

As I was leaving the National Art Gallery, I passed two guards standing outside the building. I envied the museum guards. What was it like, I wondered, to spend day after day reveling in Renoir, marveling at Matisse, wowed by Whistler?

As I walked by, I overheard one guard say to the other, "I've never seen a hummingbird." The statement startled me. He'd never seen a hummingbird? He spent his days surrounded by all that beautiful art, but he'd never seen a hummingbird.

There is a huge difference between seeing a hummingbird and seeing a picture of a hummingbird. The copy is never as good as the original. He'd never seen a real, live hummingbird. *Quel dommage,* I thought. (All that time with Monet had me thinking in French.) *What a pity.*

I've stood beak-to-beak with hummingbirds at my kitchen window. I've heard their soft thrumming approach as I sat on the deck. They've hovered so close to me that the hair on my neck prickled. I've seen their colors, their iridescent throats changing from green to ruby red to green.

I've watched a minuscule body, the size of my thumb, perched and still, drinking my homemade nectar. How can they be so tiny and live? I've seen them fight. Pugnacious, the bird book describes them. Pugnacious! Don't they realize how puny they are?

"I've never seen a hummingbird," the man said, and I pitied him. He'd never seen this stunning example of God's art in motion. God could have made all birds alike, could have stamped them out factory style. But he didn't. For the sheer delight of creating, he made a medley of light and pattern, size and shape, habit and voice. He made hummingbirds, frenzy on the wing, finer and more glorious than any still and frozen beauty crafted by man. And with that same sense of creative celebration, he made you and me.

I look at Picasso's woman. I look at myself and, after giving thanks that God is not a Cubist, I remember Psalm 139:16, "Your eyes saw my unformed body." God, the Artist, imagined me. He imagined you.

God had a vision of who you would be, exactly how he would form you. He imagined you, as a sculptor sees the finished form before he begins to chip away the stone, as a painter sees the desired result before she ever takes brush in hand. God had a vision of you before you were "knit together" in your mother's womb, and you are, the Psalmist says, "fearfully and wonderfully made" (Psalm 139:14).

Anything worth creating exacts a price from its Creator.

What does God risk in creating us? By creating us sentient and willful, he risks the creature turning its back on the Creator. By giving us freedom, God risks our rejection. We are free to spurn his company, free to go our own way. Free to take for granted or even abuse the gift of life itself. By loving us, God, like any parent, risks a broken heart.

We understand something about God by contemplating his creation. "The heavens declare the glory of God; the skies proclaim the work of his hands," says Psalm 19:1. "For since the creation of the world God's invisible qualities—his eternal power and divine nature—have been clearly seen, being understood from what has been made, so that men are without excuse" (Romans 1:20).

All of creation—hummingbirds, the gardens that inspired Monet, the sights that moved Picasso, and even us—all creation is the jubilation of God.

God imagined us, created us, made us in his image. We are connected to him. We sense the spark of hope he set in our soul. When we listen carefully, we hear his voice, whispering to our hearts. We hear the Creator calling to his creation, reaching out, and inviting intimacy. We burn as the divine breath fans hope's spark into flame, igniting our passion and giving us purpose.

And we take the leap into his arms, risking all, crying, "Yes, Lord!" and trusting him to make something beautiful of our lives.

> *It is God who works in you to will and to act according to his good purpose.*
>
> *Philippians 2:13*

 **POINTS TO PONDER**

1. Would you describe yourself as a Ming vase, a mason jar, or a clay pot? Why?

2. Describe an experience you've had with art in some form (visiting a museum, attending a play or concert, learning to paint, etc.). What moved you?

3. Complete this sentence: "I feel most creative when I . . ." Describe how it feels to be creative in this way.

Seeing Raoul

CHAPTER SIX

A permanent is, as you know if you've ever had one, only temporary. Even the Toni girls went limp after a few months. Permanent hair coloring is also only temporary. Thank goodness. I started coloring my own hair the summer between junior and senior high. The hair God gave me is a shade commonly referred to as "dishwater blonde." I'm not sure why it's called that. I've stared into countless sinks full of dishes. I've never seen my hair color.

I started coloring my hair because of those TV commercials promising, "Blondes have more fun!" Blonde was beautiful. And, my teenaged hormones raging as they were, I liked the irresistible attraction this hair color promised to inspire in the opposite sex. Witness the boys flocking around the blonde girl at the party, at the beach, or wherever else the commercial took her. I was hooked.

I bought my first home hair-coloring kit and got to work. The kit came with clear plastic gloves. I put them on, just like a surgeon. Following the instructions, I opened the small bottle and carefully added its contents to the larger bottle. I snipped the tip of the large bottle and, covering the hole with my index finger, shook the bottle to mix the two liquids. The bottle felt warmer and warmer. A chemical reaction. Wow! Real science, right there in my bathroom.

I parted my shoulder-length hair down the middle with the tip of the bottle, squeezing as I went. A line of purple goop filled the part. *Purple?* I looked at the box again, verifying the color promised was indeed "Sunshine Blonde." The little square of sample color printed on the box looked like honest-to-goodness Sandra Dee at her sunshiny blonde best.

I took a deep breath and laid another line of goop next to the first, continuing until the bottle spat its last. As directed, I massaged my scalp to spread the color, and then wrapped my hair in the clear plastic bag provided. I set the kitchen timer for the suggested twenty minutes and sat down with the latest issue of *Seventeen,* dreaming of my Sandra Dee hair and the glorious summer of blonde fun that lay ahead.

The timer dinged. I returned to the bathroom sink to rinse, shampoo, and rinse again as directed. Towel-drying my hair, I kept my eyes closed to heighten the drama of the unveiling. Facing the mirror, I opened my eyes.

My hair looked unchanged. All that work for nothing. I shook my head, tossing my locks like the lady in the commercial. I ran my fingers through my hair, lifting sections toward the light. As the hair began to dry, I saw color. Yes, color. Pale, sunshiny yellow. Glitters of silvery ash. Golden highlights! Blonde! White! Green! *Green?* I stared into the mirror, bending closer. Green. No question. But wait. What was this? I held a strand out for examination. *Pink?* Pink and green! No! This was *not* Sandra Dee!

I grabbed the box, looking closer at the color sample printed in the upper right front corner. I noticed a tiny asterisk. An asterisk couldn't be good news. I found its match in the tiny print at the bottom of the back of the box. "*Actual results may vary." *Vary?* I could have handled "vary." Slightly less than Sandra Dee drop dead gorgeous, I could have accepted. But I'd invested all my hopes and dreams—to say nothing of the dollar-twenty-nine—and ended up with this clown hair. Life was just not fair.

A very short haircut saved that summer. When anyone asked, I blamed it on a bad reaction to swimming pool chlorine. But I was more determined than ever. I was hooked on home hair coloring, drawn by the siren song of the commercials. I knew I could get it right, eventually.

I got better at it, but there were times when my hair was brassier than a proper girl's should be. And sometimes I got a little more platinum than I was aiming for. But I kept on coloring. After years of various shades of sunshine, pale blonde, yellow, gold, and brass, I decided to tame things down. I bought a darker shade. I was older. I had children. I no longer was having any fun. Why should my hair?

I followed the familiar routine, expecting familiar results— just a little tamer. It may have been my hormones, or something in the water. It may have been my hair, begging for mercy, but the result was, well, less than uniform. A little blonde, a little gold, a little white, and a little orange. Yes, orange. Like the fruit.

My son, in high school at the time, looked at my hair and said, "Interesting combination of colors you have there, Mom." This was family code. I'd taught the children, when presented with food they didn't like, to resist saying, "Yuck!" Instead, they'd learned to say, "This is an interesting combination of flavors . . ." So "interesting combination of colors" said it all. My hair was a disaster. I needed professional help. That's when I started seeing Raoul.

On my first visit to his beauty salon, Raoul assessed my situation with razor-cut precision.

"Coloring at home, are we?" he asked. I admitted I was. "Tsk, tsk, tsk!" he said. I hung my head. "And what color are we trying to be, exactly?" he asked.

"Um . . . honey blonde?" I ventured, looking up as he held several strands up for inspection.

"Really? Hmmm." He took a step back, crossed his arms, tilted his head to one side, and regarded me thoughtfully.

I tried again. "Sunshine blonde?"

Raoul furrowed his brows and shook his head. "I don't think so."

I gave it one last shot. "Sandra Dee?" I sounded pathetic and desperate and I knew it.

"How about Sandra Dee at forty-three?" he countered. It was his final offer. I agreed.

We've been coloring happily ever since. Raoul and I have an unspoken pact. Every few months, for an hour or so, he lets me pretend I'm Sandra Dee, and I let him pretend he is Vidal Sassoon. And I've thought seriously about telling my doctor that, should I be at death's door, she has permission to resuscitate me only if Raoul is available to do my retouch.

LIFE'S INTERESTING COMBINATIONS

My hair these days is an interesting combination of my natural ashy dishwater, glistening golden tones from Raoul, and God's free—and increasingly abundant—highlights of silver.

One day, as Raoul was working his magic, my friend Dora from church came into the salon. We'd both been coming to this shop for hair coloring for years, but our paths had never crossed here before. (The old commercials were right! "Does she or doesn't she? Only her hairdresser knows for sure . . .")

Dora looked at my hair, sticking out in whitish peaks from the holes in the tight rubber frosting cap (picture "Esther Williams Goes to Mars"), and said, "I had no idea you colored your hair. It always looks so natural!"

"Looking natural doesn't come so naturally anymore. It needs a little help," I said. We laughed together as Raoul's partner started laying on Dora's hair color. She was as natural a blonde as I was.

Dora said, "'Gray hair is the splendor of the old.' That's in the Bible." (Proverbs 20:29.)

I said, "Whoever wrote that obviously didn't have Raoul." We laughed some more.

Call it silly. Call it vain. I call it necessary. What Dora said next was true: "No woman ever had a bad time on a good hair day." It's like exercising and eating right—just another part of maintenance.

"Hey, it might even be good stewardship—making the most of what God gave us!" I said.

Dora confessed, "It just makes me a whole lot easier to live with. That's worth something!" We laughed but we both knew the truth. The color of our hair, the shape we're in, the lines in our faces, the numbers on the scale—all of that is deeply unimportant in the grand scheme of things. It's all just temporary.

What really matters is the permanent stuff. The sun will rise tomorrow, whether I am dishwater blonde or silvery gray or something in between. The stars will remain where he hung them, the planets will continue on course just as he planned, regardless of the changes I'm going through.

In every change—the ones we choose and the ones that choose us—God is there. In every financial struggle, every health hardship, every shattering grief, God is there. He offers predictable, dependable results. We pray, he answers. We need him, and he is there.

And God's plan for my life offers me all the colorful excitement I'll ever need. The joy of seeing him fresh in the crocuses every spring, hearing his voice on an early morning walk through the woods as he whispers, *Look over there. I have something special to show you.* The dawn breaks as I crest a hill. God raises the sun once again. I see a little more of who he really is—the unchanging, eternal God in command of all creation. For all time.

Nothing God does comes with an asterisk. His results don't vary. He has loved me with an everlasting love, through all the "interesting combinations" of my life, through all my troubles and all my triumphs.

Through it all God loves me, just as I am. That's the way he loves Dora, and that's the way he loves you, too.

I have loved you with an everlasting love;
I have drawn you with loving-kindness.

Jeremiah 31:3

POINTS TO PONDER

1. Do blondes have more fun? What do you think?

2. Have you ever had the urge to be outrageous (dye your hair purple, get a tattoo, pierce something)? Did you do it? Why or why not?

3. What are your beauty secrets?

Happy Birthday

I've started judging my friends by the birthday cards they send me. My best friends send kind sentiments, expressing appreciation for my wit and wisdom, gratitude for my friendship, and warm wishes for my continuing good health and happiness. Such cards don't whisper a word about aging.

Then there are those black balloon kind of people, those "over the hill" mockers. Their cards are all about reminding me, as if I am not already keenly aware, that I am getting older. One such card features an archaeologist type holding what looks like an ancient artifact and saying, "We found it with the Dead Sea Scrolls . . ." and inside the charming message: "And you thought your birth certificate was lost forever!"

My mother, closing in on ninety now, says she would love to get a card like that. "I knew I was getting old when I stopped getting funny cards. The cards I get now are so sweet and sappy, I'm tempted to call my doctor and ask, 'Is there something you're not telling me?'"

I shouldn't be complaining. It's nice to be remembered, even if it does come with black balloons. But what about those black balloon people with the opposite intentions—those "friends" who can't wait to burst your bubble, can't wait to rain on your parade, any time, any day.

Take Edna, for example. Edna lived across the hall from my mother on the second floor of a small apartment building. Mother was in her seventies and in good health. Edna was just a few years older but a lot slower. Any time Edna saw Mother trotting up the stairs, she'd say with a scowl, "Just you wait. When you're *my* age, you won't be trotting up those stairs!"

The years passed and Mother slowed down a little, but every chance Edna had, she'd say, "Just wait until you're *my* age. You won't be moving so fast."

When Edna was ninety-one, she was confined to bed in a nursing home. When Mother, by then well over eighty, walked in to visit her, Edna snarled, "When you're *my* age, you won't be able to walk like that! You just wait."

What is it with doomsayers like Edna? And yes, me. I've caught myself doing it. When my children were small, my childless friends would make envying noises in my direction. "This isn't as much fun as it looks," I'd say, scraping Silly Putty from my hair. "Enjoy your freedom while you can."

Later, when my children were teens, I'd feel compelled to warn young people with little children, "Enjoy them now! They aren't as much fun when they're teenagers!" I was often tempted to offer this advice in the middle of the night, when one or another of my teenagers had missed curfew and was, I was certain, "lying dead in a ditch somewhere." (I'd warned them that would happen! When they got home, I told them so!)

Now that my children are grown, I want to warn younger parents, "Enjoy them now. They'll be gone sooner than you think!" (This sentiment surfaces most often when I realize I'm the only one left at home these days to do the housework.)

The warning impulse applies to birthdays as well. I hear someone complain about turning thirty, forty, or even fifty, and I say, "What have you got to complain about? You just wait. It only gets worse."

Why do I do it? It makes me feel better somehow. I might be getting older, but at least I'm getting wiser. Or so I want them to think.

WISHFUL THINKING

We live in denial, refusing every chance we have to surrender to the enemy, to the steady march of the years. I've never heard anyone under twenty-five say they want to be younger; I've never heard anyone over twenty-five express a desire to be older. We, as a species, seem completely incapable of dealing with the reality of aging, no matter what age we are.

My sister in her sixties wishes she could be forty-five again. In my fifties, I keep thinking thirty-five was the best age to be. Our mother says she can't remember thirty-five, or sixty-five for that matter. "When I look in the mirror," she says, "I'm always so surprised to see that wrinkled face looking back. I still feel like I'm eighteen. Honest!"

Someone—a much younger person—called me "a treasure" the other day. I was horrified. Me? A treasure? I got a little huffy. "Mother Teresa was a treasure. The Queen Mum was a treasure," I said, adding in a tone that left no doubt that I had gotten wiser, not older, "I am *way too young* to be a treasure!"

What is it with us and aging? In our twenties, we declare that we will *never* be "old." In our thirties, we are sure we are finally "grown-up" and that life has just begun. At forty, we insist that we've never been better, that we're finally in our prime. At fifty, we sense we are halfway to somewhere, or maybe more than halfway. We don't really care. We just want to redecorate, or maybe just move.

At sixty, we mellow. We've never felt better, all things considered. At seventy, we'll concede to being "middle-aged," but are adamant we will never get "old." After eighty, we smile when people say we don't look our age. Of course we don't. We're still eighteen!

OF BABIES AND BIRTHDAYS

I wake up just before midnight, less than half an hour before my fifty-third birthday. I can't get back to sleep. I feel the urge to write (it happens sometimes), and to write specifically about this birthday. I want to get started on my annual birthday "inventory."

Each birthday, in a special "Birthday Thoughts" section of my journal, I write about the past year—what I've done, how life has changed. How I've changed. Noting the challenges I've met (writing this book, for instance), and the bridges I've crossed (saying goodbye to the last child). Then I ask and answer some questions: One year from today, what do I want to be writing here? What do I want to do in the next year? What goals will I set? What stretches will I attempt? (Last year I took up sketching. I'm no good at it, but I enjoy it. Last year, I accepted the fact that menopause is just around the corner, and vowed to stop fighting the inevitable.)

Eager to get started on my annual inventory, even though it's the middle of the night, I head downstairs, passing the dining room. I stop. The dining room table is bathed in dim light from the chandelier. Five gifts, wrapped and beribboned, shine on the table. Tiny foil confetti, shaped like stars and birthday hats, is strewn across the white linen tablecloth and around a vase of yellow roses, white carnations, and baby's breath. I realize that our youngest daughter, home from college, prepared this birthday surprise for me after I went to bed last night. (Wasn't it just last week when I was the one sneaking around at night after she went to bed, smuggling quarters under her pillow in exchange for lost teeth? Is she really twenty-two? Am I really going to be fifty-three?)

Several birthday cards I've received are displayed next to the gifts. I pick up the one from my mother. She had it made by a computer-savvy friend, using a picture my father took of me sometime just before my first birthday. In the picture, I'm sitting in the middle of my parents' bed wearing nothing but a diaper and a huge grin. I am reaching my arms up toward someone or something. It looks like he caught me in mid bounce.

My father called the picture "Having Fun" and entered it in his employer's Cute Baby Contest that year. (It won five dollars, which would be worth a small fortune today, had my folks had the foresight to invest it for me. But I forgive them. They had mouths to feed. Mine chief among them.)

I stare at the picture, thinking about that baby, about the fact that I am the same person, fifty-three years later. I do seem to be "having fun," just as the caption says. Am I still "having fun"?

I wonder what time I was born. Was it morning or afternoon, or was I a middle-of-the-night arrival, as babies often are? I have my birth certificate. I could check the time. Was the labor long and difficult? Was my mother awake? I can call her later and ask. What time was I born, historically? What was the news on that day? I could check the library newspaper archives for the headlines.

It's easy enough to find out the facts, but the feelings are harder to get at, hidden behind the cloud of time.

I was born smack in the middle of America's postwar reveling, on the wave of relief that came with surviving a long war. It was the end of the war that sent boys into battle, drunk with confidence, to be quickly sobered by war's harsh reality. They came home with nightmares, hungry for dreams, wanting the solace of good wives in warm beds, and the hope of peace for their sweet babies. And we were born by the thousands daily, crowding the hospitals and later the schools. We were the Baby Boom.

I look at the picture and think about the man on the other side of the Brownie box camera, looking down into its viewfinder. I imagine the woman standing at his left, coaxing the baby to smile. The baby squeals and kicks her legs, bouncing on the mattress. The woman laughs encouragement, and the baby laughs louder, smiles bigger, reaches farther, and kicks harder, just as the man presses the shutter, capturing joy in the box.

The mother bends down then and scoops the baby into loving arms. The man turns and wraps strong arms around them both. Holding them. Holding them. This is the father's reward, well-earned for having saved the world from tyranny. His own personal baby boom caught in black and white on this day long ago, in this moment, "having fun."

MOMENTS IN TIME

Years later, I watched a video made from an old 8mm home movie, taken on a sunny Sunday in a park where my father's family gathered for a picnic. I watched the silent pictures of my aunts and uncles—fourteen of them total—as the camera panned their smooth, round faces. I watched the video closely—rewinding it several times to the moment after my uncle Carl smiled, after my aunt Helen held a shy hand before her face. That was the moment I glimpsed my father's face.

In that long ago moment, he glanced right to his sister, then up to the camera, then back to her again. A glance right, up, right again. Just a moment. A moment when I was a toddler, before he got older, before he had cancer. Before I was in high school and watched him wasting away in the living room. I rewound and replayed the tape again and again, holding him there in that moment when he was still well, still young.

That moment when he was alive.

Once upon a time, a long time ago, we sat in a diaper in the middle of a bed, laughing, reaching, open and alive. We grew and learned to move from springs to summers to falls to winters, navigating the seasons and negotiating the changes. Gradually, we laughed less. Slowly, we pulled back our reach, risking less. By increments, we closed parts of ourselves off from the world, from pain. In a hundred small ways, we died slowly, year by year. Why, we wonder, looking back. What were we so afraid of? What got in our way? Who told us we could not, should not, dare not?

Was it Edna? Or were we our own worst enemy, crushing our own dreams, giving in to our own fears?

THE GIFT OF MOMENTS

Each year, each day, each moment is a gift from God. Each birthday is a milestone and cause for celebration. Birthdays are the perfect time to pause and reflect. A time to ask not only "Where have I been?" but "Where am I headed?" Not just "What have I accomplished?" but also "Who am I becoming?" Birthdays bring the blessing of a fresh start, new possibilities, and fresh dreams. And birthdays are a time to remember.

This year I think about the baby on the bed and the man who took her picture, who later taught her to love words, poetry, and music. I think about the woman who encouraged her and made her laugh—who still makes her laugh—and I am grateful. Grateful for memories that are worth keeping, grateful for the forgiveness and healing God offers for the memories I'm not so glad to have.

This year I realize I'm exactly as old as God intended me to be, given the date of my birth. Who am I to argue with God? "Teach us to number our days aright, that we may gain a heart of wisdom," I pray with the psalmist (Psalm 90:12). He who numbered my days ordained them all before one of them came to be. He wrapped for us the gift of years, the gift of days, the gift of moments. Each granted, each ordained by a sovereign, loving God.

What time was I born? In God's perfect time.

> *But I trust in you, O L*ORD*;*
> *I say, "You are my God."*
> *My times are in your hands.*
>
> *Psalm 31:14–15*

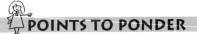

POINTS TO PONDER

1. Who is the Edna in your life?

2. Describe your happiest birthday memory. What was your saddest birthday? What was missing that year? What was (or will be) the toughest birthday for you?

3. What does it mean to be "young at heart"? Are you?

Northern Girls: A Tribute

I got dressed for church one Sunday morning last March. Here in the North Country, March is the month when winter makes up for any kindness it's reluctantly granted over the previous months. March is when the air masses collide and wreak all kinds of weather havoc. Massive snowstorms come mixed with freezing rain, sleet, and hail. Thunder and lightning come with the snow. It's a confusing time in weather, and in fashion, for Northern Girls.

We long to put our turtlenecks and heavy sweaters into storage. We are eager to wash our mittens, scarves, and knit stocking caps and stow them away for the season. We are itching to pack away the down jackets and send our ankle-length black wool coats to the cleaners, but we know better. Doing any of these things will guarantee a blizzard within twenty-four hours (much like washing our car in the summer guarantees rain). So we wait, bored with our wardrobe, continuing to bundle ourselves in warm flannels and scratchy wools as we dream of pastels and short sleeves.

On this particular sleety Sunday, I pulled on my sagging long johns one more time. (These are not the sleek and shiny long underwear I've seen advertised in exclusive catalogs. These are heavy-duty, cold-fighting thermals. Add a drop seat and I could be your grandpa.) Then, in a moment of fashion desperation, I pawed through my closet, shoving aside all my heavy black, gray, and brown (fully lined for extra warmth, naturally) slacks. I searched frantically for anything that would lighten the heavy winter fashion mood and give me some hope of spring.

In the back corner of the closet, I found a pair of pale peach silk slacks. I slipped them on. The delicate fabric of the slacks couldn't hide the bulk of the long johns, but I didn't care. The silky pants cried out for strappy, high-heeled sandals, but mine, which I had worn once to a wedding six years before, were packed away. I put on my heavy wool socks and hiking boots. I knew I was a huge fashion "DON'T!" but I had no choice. Freezing rain was falling. Paris might have been showing "sleek and sexy," but "traction" is the watchword for our spring season.

I am a Northern Girl. While we may not be hot in the fashion sense, we evidently have, according to the Beach Boys at least, hot lips. Our kisses, they crooned, keep our boyfriends warm at night. This is much appreciated most of the year, but doesn't do us much good in January. Overnight temperatures drop well below zero, causing lips—even hot ones—to freeze on contact with any surface. Pop cans. Car doors. Other lips. (Try explaining all this to your father when you get home from your date two hours late, and he's waiting in the living room for you— with his Bible in one hand and his shotgun in the other.)

But hot lips aren't much consolation when spring finally comes and, after nine months in hibernation, we emerge from our caves, shedding layer after layer of clothing. We discover that we've added a few more layers of our own, which can't be so easily shed. Thanks to too little physical movement (it's important to conserve energy in the winter) and too many hearty winter Sunday dinners, our thighs have turned to squishy, dimpled masses of flesh. We're sporting our own dumplings, just south of the border.

Northern Girls. For nine months each year, our lives revolve around the weather. Beginning in September and continuing through May, we answer all invitations with, "I'll be there . . . weather permitting." An early snow, before we've dug the snow blower out from the back corner of the garage, can hold us prisoner in our driveway for days. A late snow, if we've been foolish enough to put the snow blower away before June, can drive us mad.

Even at the height of summer, we pay winter homage. Our local parade features a group carrying snow shovels. They dance along the parade route pretending to scoop and swoop, dig and toss. The shovel blades thunk and scrape against the street; the steel, swinging high over the shoulder, glints in the sun. This is our native dance. This group is our version of a drum and bugle corps. Their rhythm is in our blood.

We've been performing the ritual movements since childhood. Some of us actually enjoy shoveling. Lulled by the repetitive motion, we use the time to ponder the big questions of life: *Will*

Aunt Maudie make a fuss at Christmas again this year? Will we have to call the police again? Where did I leave the rake last fall? Is that it sticking out of that snowbank over there?

HEAT WAVES

Not everybody lives like this, I realized, when I moved to southern California for a few years. California has sunshine. Relentless sunshine. After a while, I started longing for rainy days so I could stay indoors without feeling guilty. Northern Girls learn early to spend every nice day outside. We never know when we'll have another one.

Endless summer got a little tedious. I felt I had to keep on having fun. I longed for signs of fall, signs I'd learned to interpret from infancy to mean, "End of vacation. Party's over. Time to buckle down and get to work." I longed for cold snaps that would make me want to curl up in front of a fire with a good book. I wanted real fire; we had a fireplace with a gas starter (that's cheating) and we bought our wood at the supermarket. A bundle of six sorry little shrink-wrapped sticks for a dollar forty-nine. Burning it generated more stench than warmth. It was a sad, sad substitute for North Country ambiance.

The hardest thing about living in California was living among all those California girls. "The cutest girls in the world," the Beach Boys sang. It was true. No wonder the Beach Boys wished we "all could be California girls." These girls were perky, energetic, and fashionable. And thin. I ran into Malibu Barbie everywhere I turned.

I just didn't belong. When my thighs couldn't take the pressure any longer, I moved back home. Rhoda Morgenstern said she moved from New York to Minneapolis because she figured she'd keep better in the cold. She had a good point. She neglected to mention the other advantage of cold weather: layered clothing. Nobody can tell what size you really are under three sweaters and a parka.

My first month back home in the North Country, on a delightfully brisk November day, a guy named Vern delivered a pickup truck load of firewood to my front yard. (This was a little embarrassing, since we'd bought a house on six acres of woods. I tried to explain to Vern that we hadn't had time to buy a chain saw yet. I think I heard him muttering, "Carrying coals to Newcastle," or maybe it was, "Selling ice to the Eskimos." Or maybe he said he'd be "laughing all the way to the bank." I don't recall exactly.)

After Vern dropped that load of wood on the front lawn, I layered myself in sweater and jacket, long johns and jeans, woolly socks and hiking boots, and headed outside. Despite wearing gloves, I lost every one of my fake California fingernails, and five pounds, hauling and stacking the wood in the backyard. Then I trudged through the forest around the house gathering kindling, carrying the dry sticks and twigs in a leather sling I'd picked up at the Army-Navy surplus store for just this purpose.

I split a few pieces of Vern's wood with my ax, and hauled it into the house. I laid the split wood carefully across the kindling I'd piled in the living room fireplace, in a crisscross pattern so beautiful it would have brought a tear to any Scoutmaster's eye.

I stuffed crumpled newspaper around the pile, struck a wooden match against the seam in my jeans, and lit the fire. It flickered a few times, then roared to life. (Take that, Malibu Barbie!)

The living room was toasty in no time. In fact, the fire I built—without cheating—soon generated enough heat to drive any woman over fifty from the room in three minutes flat. Which is why I watched it from the kitchen. I sat and enjoyed that fire, sipping a hot cup of cocoa with marshmallows and picking fuzzy burdocks from my wool socks—souvenirs from my trek in the woods. As I picked I sang, "Take me home, country roads . . ."

Ahh. This was North Country ambiance. My favorite kind of heat wave. It was good to be home.

OH, PIONEERS!

Northern Girls. We are sturdy stock from sturdy foremothers—the women who tamed the frontier. They rode weeks in a wagon, creating new lives out of nothing, in the wilderness. All without a bathtub, without makeup, without deodorant. No curling irons, no hair gel, no mirrors. Perhaps having no mirrors was a blessing.

How did they do it? They had no beepers, no cell phones, no DayTimers, and no Palm Pilots. How did they manage? How did they learn to make hotdish? How did they organize the first coffee klatsch? Did Pony Express carry the message? "Let's all get together at Inga Olson's house on Thursday. Better make that six weeks from Thursday. It will take us that long to get there."

They didn't need aerobics classes. Not when they had to walk across forty acres to get to the back fence to chat with the neighbor lady. They did it without circuit training and without heart-rate monitors. No Spandex shorts or sweatbands, no walking shoes designed for proper arch support, no little air bubbles in the soles for tired feet to ride on.

No wonder they look so tired in their pictures, those poor pioneer ladies. *How old do you suppose Great Grandmother is in this picture? She looks about sixty . . .* You do some research and discover that's Baby John on her lap. He is her fourth child. You do the math. She's twenty-three years old! *And she's able to sit up? Now that's the pioneer spirit!*

WOMEN OF THE EARTH

I read a poem recently about three Southern women; it described their grace, beauty, and softness. I chuckled, thinking of the contrast with my own Northern grandmother. I imagined the scene . . .

Grandma and two of her friends stand together outside on a long-ago Sunday in July, in a yard somewhere near here. They are gathered that day to enjoy a visit. They don't get to visit with each other very often, busy as they are with chores and children.

They are solid women, dressed up for the occasion in their muted print dresses and their black tie shoes with the small heels—what we always called "Grandma shoes." Their long cotton stockings are rolled down to their ankles. It's too hot for stockings. One woman raises her hand to shield her eyes against the sun; the back of her upper arm flaps gently in the breeze.

They talk together there on the sparse grass of the front yard, the big white clapboard-sided farmhouse behind them. The long dusty driveway stretches a hundred yards from nowhere to meet the gravel road that goes everywhere else.

These women are bound here, bound to the land as certainly as the hens will lay. They talk here of children and housework, farm chores and news. Their only connection with the world is here on this plot with each other, and the bits of news they've picked up from their men, who've been to town. They are women of the earth. They are tied here, tied to the men, to the family, to the land. And they wouldn't have it any other way.

My grandmother never went to therapy. When she was stressed, she scrubbed the floor. She had ten children. She had very clean floors. When I was three weeks overdue with my first baby, my mother advised, "Try scrubbing the floor. It always worked for your grandmother." I tried it. It worked.

Grandma kept things simple. When someone was hurt she said, "I'm sorry you're hurt," and made them hotdish. When bad things happened to people she cared about, she didn't feel compelled to make it all better. She said, "That's too bad," and made them hotdish.

When her children had birthdays, she didn't feel the need to treat a hundred neighborhood kids to a day at the local amusement park in celebration. She said, "Happy Birthday," made a cake, and (you guessed it) made a hotdish.

Grandma loved to knit, and she kept knitting mittens, by feel, long after she was too blind to see what she was doing. She'd hold up the work, asking my mother, in Finnish, to check it for holes. When my mother guided her fingers to the holes she'd made, Grandma would laugh. She loved to knit. Holes didn't matter.

STURDY GIRLS

Grandma and her friends were Northern Girls. And so am I.

So, we're not admired for our "hip" fashion sense, like those Eastern girls. We don't purr when we talk, like the Southern girls. We kiss well, which is fine because that's done with eyes closed. We're beautiful that way. (With his eyes closed, a guy could be kissing a California girl for all he knows. We appreciate that.) We may not be fashionable or sweet-talking, but we are sturdy.

I heard of one Northern Girl whose husband's pet name for her was "Hay Bale." She considered it high praise. He bought her a new shotgun one Christmas. The next deer-hunting season, while he was out in the woods killing nothing, she took down a buck from the front porch, gutted it, and had it hanging in the front yard when he came back. And she still had time to do the laundry, balance the checkbook, and fix dinner, without breaking a sweat. Now that's sturdy. And practical.

Northern Girls are very practical. We don't like a fuss, even at Christmas. We enjoy getting a new blender or a new vacuum cleaner, but to really get our hearts fluttering, a new chain saw is the ticket. If we do get something personal, we don't need the pink satin from Victoria's Secret; those things are far too revealing of what we spend our lives trying to hide. Something oversized in flannel from Wal-Mart will do just fine. Our favorite color? Plaid.

We are practical. As Inga Olson wrote in *Northern Girls: Practically a Handbook:* "A Northern Girl is a sturdy, solid, sensible girl. But for those of you from other places, don't worry about it. Being a Northern Girl has nothing to do with geography. It's a matter of the heart. Just be practical. Just be there. You'll get the hang of it."

If you need us, we are there. Northern Girls of legend have driven two hundred miles in blizzards to reach a parent, child, sister, or brother in need. One Northern Girl's mother was in the hospital for two weeks, dangerously ill. The daughter sat vigil at her bedside until she recovered. It's what a Northern Girl does.

Another Northern Girl's mother had terminal cancer. The mother, being a practical Northern Girl herself, planned her own funeral, asking to be laid out in her fanciest dress. "Isn't it a little too fancy?" a friend asked. The mother said it wasn't at all too fancy; she was, after all, "going to meet the King!"

In the last days, the daughter took care of her mother, bathing her, giving her medication, praying with her, holding her until the end. Her own eighteen-year-old daughter, one of the next generation of Northern Girls, was right beside her doing her part. How could they do it? They must have taken to heart the Northern Girl's creed, which Jesus explained like this: "In this world you will have trouble. But take heart! I have overcome the world" (John 16:33).

Inga Olson the pioneer was right. Northern Girls are practical. Are you hungry? We'll make you hotdish. Thirsty? The coffee pot is always on at our house. Sick? We'll bring you turkey soup. Lonely? We've always got time to talk as we fold laundry.

Cold? We've got an afghan on every piece of furniture in the house, even in the middle of August. In jail? We'll stop by on our way home from the bakery and bring you doughnuts. I'll bet if the Beach Boys had gotten to know more Northern Girls, they'd have been singing a different tune.

It's like Jesus said: "For I was hungry and you gave me something to eat, I was thirsty and you gave me something to drink, I was a stranger and you invited me in, I needed clothes and you clothed me, I was sick and you looked after me, I was in prison and you came to visit me" (Matthew 25:35–36).

He must have known some Northern Girls.

> *"I tell you the truth, whatever you did for one of the least of these . . . you did for me."*
>
> *Matthew 25:40*

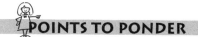

POINTS TO PONDER

1. Do you know a "Northern Girl"? Describe her. Where in her do you see the qualities of mercy, compassion, or a "servant heart"?

2. Have you experienced a life-threatening illness or the death of someone close to you? How has the experience affected you?

3. What did Jesus mean when he said, "Whatever you did for the least of these . . . you did for me" (Matthew 25:40)?

Women of History

I've never made headlines or been on the front page of the newspaper. I've never held political office. I'll never be a household name. Nobody will ever build a statue in my honor, dedicate a hospital wing to my memory, or name a city after me. I'll never be famous, and, God willing, I'll never be infamous like Ma Barker or Lizzie Borden. I won't be on anyone's "Most Wanted" list. I won't be seeing my picture at the post office.

Yet, I am a woman of history. I subscribe to an on-line newsletter (www.historyswomen.com) that comes addressed "To History's Women." The newsletter profiles women who've had an impact on world events, overcoming obstacles to achieve great things. Women like temperance leader Frances Willard, activist Ida Wells-Barnett, and the abolitionist Grimke sisters. I got to thinking about some other women of the past who, in midlife, made unique contributions to history. The accomplishments of these premenopausal and PMS pioneers probably won't be lauded in any newsletters, so I'll mention them here.

There was Martha Washington, who borrowed from George and penned, "I cannot tell a lie. Middle age stinks." On her fiftieth birthday, she was heard to shout, "Out of my way, George, I need to redecorate Mount Vernon!" She is rumored to have invented sponge painting and crackle finishes, launching a do-it-yourself home improvement frenzy that continues to this day. Martha Stewart is named after her.

Artist's model Venus Johnson, of Milo, Italy, was obviously menopausal the day she snapped at the sculptor. "Arms up, arms down. Cross the arms, don't cross the arms. Make up your stupid mind!" The rest, as they say, is history.

It was Mrs. Robert E. Lee who first said, "Is it hot in the South, or is it just me?" And we shouldn't forget the six Lipnitz sisters of Cleveland, all of whom hit menopause within a three-year span. This inspired their brother Bernard, the only boy in the family, to invent the theory of global warming at the National Institutes of Science.

"What was Bernie supposed to think?" shrugged his oldest sister, Estelle. "All of us flashing at once melted the shingles right off the roof."

It's not widely known that it was Caesar's wife, Julia, who actually invented the calendar, at her husband's request. "Julius wanted to know when each month he should plan to go off conquering cooler territory." Historians blame her for the Gallic Wars, particularly the Winter Rebellion of 54 b.c., during which Julia coined the term "cabin fever."

And long before that, Eve is rumored to have been the first to say, "Fig leaf, schmig leaf! Where are the Depends? And could you turn it down a little in this garden? I'm dying here!"

Then there was Abraham's wife, Sarah, the first woman on record to give birth to a "surprise" midlife baby. When she got the news, she didn't shriek at the angel, "What do you mean I'm pregnant! Where did you get your medical degree? From a Wheaties box?"

No, Sarah didn't freak out. She laughed and made a little joke. "After I'm worn out . . . will I now have this pleasure?" (Genesis 18:12). She called it a "pleasure." This is the first sarcastic remark ever recorded.

Sarah had to have heard about the rib-battering, bladder-bouncing "pleasure" of being a human Hilton for nine months. She had surely heard about the "pleasure" of two A.M. feedings, colic, spit-up, and mountains of laundry. She knew about the joy of dark circles under the eyes, stretch marks, "baby fat" that never goes away, and breasts that sag navel-ward.

The Bible says Sarah got the news and laughed. Maybe it was just gas.

LEAVING A LEGACY

We are all making history. We're leaving a legacy. What is yours? What impact are you having on world events? On your personal world? How will you be remembered? Imagine some-one writing your biography a hundred years from now. What would they be saying about you?

I imagine mine might be something like this: "She was a practical woman. She hardly ever whined about getting older and losing her shape. She didn't complain too awfully much about her aches and pains.

"She was a passable cook, though it's been recorded that her husband said once, 'Are you cooking something or is something burning? Oh, wait. That's redundant.' Which is why they usually ate in restaurants, where she was a very good listener. She was able to hear three conversations at once, except the one at her own table.

"She was a wonderful mother. Her children hardly ever had to wait in line to talk to her while she was busy writing. When they grew up, she never said, 'You never call me.' Well, hardly ever.

"Asked what her tombstone should say, she thought about requesting 'Well, at least she tried,' but she opted for 'I told you I was sick!' instead."

THE CHANGING OF THE GUARD

One day we will all pass into history. We'll be gone from this world. There will be a "changing of the guard." (That's a euphemism for death. I won't mention the others like expiring, kicking the bucket, buying the farm, pushing up daisies, passing on, or passing away.)

A complete changing of the guard was recorded when Moses took a census. Not one of the original Israelites who set out from Egypt lived to enter the Promised Land (Numbers 26:64–65). One generation dies; the next steps up to take over. And the next. One day, no one will be alive who lived through the

Depression, or World War II. One day no one will be alive who fought in the Vietnam War, or the Gulf War, or witnessed the horrifying events of September 11, 2001.

Are we really "here today, gone tomorrow," and forgotten the next? Forty years after his passing, I still remember my father. I remember how he smelled—a blend of fresh-cut wood and Old Spice. I remember his nicked and gnarled carpenter hands and the pressed crease of his khaki work pants. I remember him standing in a swirl of sawdust in his workshop, pushing oak planks through the table saw. I remember his smile.

He was a tall, strong man, which made the hollowing that happened with his cancer all the more terrible. I remember the sad look of his leaving, the resigned hang of his red cardigan sweater over his gaunt frame as he walked out the back door. I remember so much, four decades later. I still miss him. Who will miss him forty years from now?

Given current actuarial probabilities, not one Baby Boomer will be around a hundred years from now. But we are here today, in the driver's seat. That magnificent generation of Great Depression survivors, freedom fighters, and tamers of the suburban wilderness, who secured our cushy future by their hard work, are ready to take it easy. They're ready for us to run things, but are we ready for the responsibility?

When the first Baby Boomer got elected president of the United States, I told my husband, "Politics aside, I feel like our parents just died and our doofy older brother is now in charge of the family. I'm scared!"

Aren't we the generation that never wanted to grow up? I don't think we should be entrusting the future of the free world to anyone who wore love beads or a macramé vest, or had a wall decoration constructed from the metal tabs from pop-top cans. Knowing all the words to the Beach Boys' *Endless Summer* album hardly qualifies a person to lead the nation. When the ship of state starts to sink, how reassuring will it be to hear the president say, "No sweat, man. I can do The Swim. And my Bugaloo isn't bad either."

Who put us in charge? How will I feel when my children are in control? It's bad enough having a president who's my age. How will I feel when she is younger than I am? I'm getting used to the dentist and the doctor being my juniors, but the president? Scary. Very scary.

THE UNBROKEN CHAIN

We're all making history, influencing our worlds. The women of history are the women who get up in the middle of the night to rock a restless toddler back to sleep. The women who attend every band concert, every dance recital, and every play performance to encourage and applaud. They are the women who make the cookies, bring the bars, and supply the salads for countless funeral lunches. They clean and organize the kitchens and sew the quilts for the fund-raisers. The women of history are the women who quietly make their homes welcoming havens for their weary families.

They are the women who temper corporate life with grace, manage foundations, teach classes, and provide counseling.

They are the women who pray for the wisdom and courage to say "no" when it's necessary, and to say "yes" with confidence when the timing is right.

The women who say, "Trust God. Wait and hope," when the future looks grimmest.

The women who say, "I'm here," when everyone else has jumped ship.

The unsung heroes are the women who train the women, who will train the next generation of women, to keep caring, keep trying, keep mending fences, keep bridging gaps of love and communication. To keep trusting, to keep praying, to "keep on keeping on," because that's what women do.

These are the women of history and this is their legacy—this unbroken chain of women through the ages, caring, showing up, and doing what's needed.

I read the other day, "Watch your children as they grow up. They will teach you what you have taught them." We are leaving a legacy day by day, in the tenderness and compassion we demonstrate, in the love we share and extend to the unlovable, in our generosity of spirit, and in our tolerance of human imperfection. In our willingness to forgive, to accept, to surrender our rights and our wills for the sake of others.

The guard will be changing soon. Let's not waste time, then. Let's do all the good we can do while we can. Before the nursing home, before the catastrophic illness, before we forget. Take time to hug, to laugh. Change someone's life. Smile. Encourage. Give a little. Forgive a lot. Call an old friend. Mend a fence.

You never know what tomorrow will bring. We have only today, this moment. Savor it. Life is short. Live.

Make some history.

> *And God is able to make all grace abound to you, so that in all things at all times, having all that you need, you will abound in every good work.*
>
> *2 Corinthians 9:8*

POINTS TO PONDER

1. What famous woman do you most admire and why?

2. How would you like to be remembered by your family? Your friends? Your coworkers? (Write the speeches they'll be giving at your funeral!)

3. Have you ever wanted to be famous? If so, describe the Fabulously Famous You who lives in this fantasy. What is the price of fame?

Martha, Martha, Mary, and Me

The superstars of American womanhood are those we call by their first names only: Cher. Oprah. Martha. I recently met the only woman in America who doesn't know Martha Stewart; she'd just returned from twelve years in Vietnam.

I got hooked on Martha Stewart's TV show one week when I was redecorating my dining room. I don't usually watch daytime television, but I turned it on for company while I was wallpapering and painting. I learned so much in a week of watching Martha. On Monday, she taught me how to have fun with fennel. I had never actually owned fennel before, but I added it to my shopping list for that week.

On Tuesday, Martha showed me how to bake Boscs. I thought Boscs were some kind of French people, but they are evidently some kind of pear. (Who knew?) As Martha demonstrated Bosc baking, I realized how very important it was for me to learn how to do this. My family and friends, Martha assured me, would love me for it. My life in general would improve if I did this. I vowed to bake my own Boscs soon—very soon. I added them to my shopping list.

On Wednesday, Martha made one of her perfect desserts. She said, as she added the honey, "This is from my own hive." *What a woman!* I thought and then, *Oh mercy! I wonder what she'll do if the recipe calls for eggs.*

On Thursday, Martha turned an old beat-up antique chair into a vision of beauty. She stripped the wood until all vestiges of age were gone. Then she stained it and added just the right aging touches back into it. She created a perfectly aged antique, one that looked more authentic, more perfectly aged than the original had. I added this to my to-do list:

1. Buy antique something and make it more perfectly antique.
2. Figure out how to apply this "aging perfectly" process to self.

Later on Thursday, Martha took me on a tour of her perfect garden. (Some mean person said that Martha's passion for "forcing" bulbs to bloom proves she's a control freak. They were probably just jealous.) It's no wonder Martha's garden yields perfect flowers and perfect produce. Her compost (I hesitate to call it a "pile") is beautiful. Beautiful.

By Friday, after a week of Marthazation, I was exhausted. Guilt gnawed at me. I was obviously a homemaking disaster. I had no antiques, real or remanufactured. I'd never made my own marshmallows, though a friend did, following Martha's recipe. Yield: three marshmallows. Cost: $16.99 each, including the cost of replacing her mixer after the motor burned out trying to fluff the sticky mess.

I was a failure. I bought my sheets—pardon me, "bed linens"—at the local discount store when I should have been weaving them myself from cotton I'd grown, organically of course, on the back forty. And I didn't even iron them when I changed the beds.

I also realized I had been a terrible mother. All those years, I'd sent my children to school with plain old peanut butter and jelly sandwiches in their brown bag lunches. I should have spread home-ground peanuts and home-canned preserves on two thick slabs of home-baked bread, on which I'd painted a likeness of George Washington Carver. More original art—an *art nouveau* peanut plant perhaps, or a map of antebellum Georgia—should have decorated the handmade paper bag.

I was a mess! My craft supplies were strewn about the house, not neatly organized in an antique cupboard designed specifically for this purpose. I didn't have a drawer full of decorative stamping supplies and colorful stickers and a thousand-foot roll of butcher paper at the ready, should a gift-wrapping emergency befall me.

I was no better outdoors than in. Aphids carried off my lone rose bush, moles devoured my tulip bulbs, and the squirrels got the zucchini. My mulch disappeared with the first good rain, and my compost heap was, well, just a heap. My garden was full of (gasp!) dirt. Oh, the angst!

I just couldn't imagine how one woman could do it all. Or why she'd want to, for that matter. I was hopeless. I slid deeper and deeper into the funk of futility until forty-five minutes into Friday's show. That's when I saw the commercial for a CD called "Polka! Polka! Polka!" and its companion CD, "Everybody Polka!"

Reality check! a little voice in my head said. *Snap out of it!* My feet started dancing the one-two-three of the polka, a beat I'd been moving to since infancy. When Martha returned to the screen I shook my paint-encrusted fist at her; I hadn't had time to buy the case of surgical gloves Martha recommended for painting projects.

"I give up, Martha!" I hollered at the TV. "I'm from the Midwest. We're just plain folks. We don't Bosc. We don't Anjou. We're Bartlett people. We buy 'em green, stick 'em in a brown paper bag to ripen, and put the bag on top of the refrigerator. We forget about it. Several weeks later, we discover the bag, look inside, and say, 'Oh, dear. I think these once were pears,' and toss them out. If we wanted to do stuff with fresh fruit, we'd move to California."

ANOTHER TIME, ANOTHER MARTHA

Later that day, after I'd calmed down, I was reading the Bible story of another Martha in Luke 10:38–41:

> As Jesus and his disciples were on their way, he came to a village where a woman named Martha opened her home to him. She had a sister called Mary, who sat at the Lord's feet listening to what he said. But Martha was distracted

by all the preparations that had to be made. She came to him and asked, "Lord, don't you care that my sister has left me to do the work by myself? Tell her to help me!"

"Martha, Martha," the Lord answered, "you are worried and upset about many things, but only one thing is needed. Mary has chosen what is better, and it will not be taken away from her."

I feel bad for Martha. She was working her fool head off trying to make things nice for her company, and she got scolded for it. She was just trying to make a good impression. Was that so bad? Who could blame her? It's not every day Jesus drops by for coffee.

"Don't be such a Martha!" I've heard women say to each other. "She's a real Martha" is an insult these days, whether it's referring to the Bible Martha or the one on TV. Why? The implication is that the woman is so absorbed in the details of daily life, trying so hard to have everything just right, that she is missing what's important.

Being "a real Martha" implies that she has no time for what really matters because she is so busy fussing over frivolities. I have to confess that the things I get all worked up about are all too often (not to put too fine a point on it) deeply unimportant. *Should I cut my hair shorter? Should I paint the dining room mauve or periwinkle? Should I serve orange roughy or salmon steaks for dinner?* In the grand scheme of things, who cares? As my father was fond of saying, "Nobody is going to know the difference a hundred years from now." Or ten years from now. Or maybe even tomorrow.

Jesus said to Martha, "You are worried and upset about many things." He wasn't condemning her for wanting to feed her company, or make things ready for them. It was the *worry* that Jesus keyed in on. Martha was wearing blinders of worry; she probably didn't see that all the fussing and fuming might actually be making her guests uncomfortable. Have you ever had dinner at the home of someone who is so busy fussing that they never have time to sit and visit?

Martha was intensely focused on getting things done. How intensely focused can I be? Ask me that question when it's time for my favorite program on television. Ask me when I have two hours to shop and ten gifts to buy. Ask me when I've sunk into the latest novel from my favorite mystery writer. (I won't hear you, but you can ask.) Ask me when I'm finishing the vacuuming as the dinner guests are pulling into the driveway, or when I'm in the middle of closet cleaning, or when I'm rushing to get six hundred tulip bulbs planted before the snow flies.

If God whispered my name at that moment, could I stop what I'm doing and sit at his feet? Would I be able to be like Mary in the middle of being Martha?

Jesus keyed in on the fact that Martha was worried and upset. That worry kept her from seeing the bigger picture. Martha whined (I'm sorry Martha, but you *were* whining) and I paraphrase, "How come my sister isn't helping me? Why do I always have to do all the work?" I wonder if Martha said the same things to their mother as she and Mary were growing up. Was she always a whiner? Martha obviously had some "issues."

Martha was distracted, worried, and upset. But the way she asks, "Lord, don't you care . . . ?" tugs at my heart. I feel her pain. She was working hard. I wonder if she didn't just want to hear Jesus say, "Martha, you don't have to work so hard to try to impress me or to please me. I love you regardless of what you do for me. Sit down here and rest."

Maybe that's what Jesus wanted Martha to understand when he said, "Only one thing is needed." Only one thing is necessary. One thing. One. And Mary had figured it out.

ONLY ONE THING

What is that "one thing" for all of us? Let's look at what it is *not*.

The one thing we need is not a new to-do list loaded with nobler, more spiritual things to do. It's not a new time management technique, not a new organizational planner, not a class in resource management, or a new computer calendar program.

That one thing—the one truly *necessary* thing Jesus was talking about—is time with God.

I've attended many seminars on life management skills. I've studied countless books promising me more fulfillment through more efficient living, through proper goal setting, through the latest in self-improvement philosophy.

One program suggested, "Picture your life as a bicycle wheel." I did. I pictured myself in the center of the wheel. Radiating out on the spokes were all my areas of need and responsibility: job, family, volunteering, finances, physical needs, emotional needs, social and intellectual needs. These were the spokes of my life.

Then they asked, "How satisfied are you with each spoke?"
I placed a black dot on each spoke—near the center of the wheel
to indicate little satisfaction in that area, out at the rim of the
wheel to indicate perfect satisfaction with that area of my life.

"Connect your dots." I connected the marks to reveal the
shape of my "life wheel." My life's wheel looked like a bicycle
tire that had been run over by a semi. What a lumpy mess! The
experts told me to set goals in each area to bring all my dots into
a smooth, rounded balance.

I tried. Really I did. But just when I started making progress
on my physical goals, my family goals were falling apart. When
I started spending more time with my family, my career goals
suffered. Before long, my bicycle wheel felt more like a gerbil
wheel; I was running as fast as I could and getting nowhere.

Why was it so impossible for me to get that wheel rounded
out and keep it that way? Because the self-helpers had me dead-
ended. The problem wasn't that my spokes were bad; all my
goals were honorable and noble.

The problem was at the *hub* of the wheel. Little old me, one
little gerbil all by myself in the middle of that wheel—I didn't
have the strength, courage, self-discipline, wisdom, energy,
power, and commitment it took to keep a life going for the long
haul. I have only 168 hours in a week, not enough time to do all
I dream of doing, or need to do, to keep the wheel of my life
rolling smoothly.

The one thing I was missing is the *one thing* I really need.
"Only one thing is needed," Jesus said. That "one thing" is God.

I took "spiritual needs" off the spoke and put it at the *center* of the wheel. My spiritual life isn't just another "area" for me to set goals in. My spiritual life is the *hub* of the wheel, the part that keeps everything else turning. Everything else in my life revolves around my relationship with God.

That made all the difference. "God first" is the only necessary thing. With God at the center, the rest of my life falls into place. Just like the Bible says: "He is before all things, and in him all things hold together" (Colossians 1:17).

GOD FIRST

I can still "Martha" with the best of them. And the truth is, without the Marthas of the world, a lot of committees would fall apart. PTAs across the land would fold. There'd be no more church picnics, no more potlucks, no more class parties. There'd be no more do-it-yourself industry. Home improvement stores would go bankrupt.

I've cooked and cleaned, served and hosted with the best. And the work has often been a blessing to me. But what blesses me most is the fact that God loved me before I did a single thing.

When Jesus said, "Mary has chosen what is better," he meant that she had recognized and chosen the one *necessary* thing: God first. She chose to focus on who had come to call, to sit down and listen to what he had to say, *before* she got busy trying to serve him.

I don't want to be so busy washing the supper dishes that I miss the beautiful sunset God has splashed across the western sky. I don't want to be banging pots in the kitchen and miss the sound of his voice, rumbling low, calling me to the living room, *Come here, I have something to tell you . . .*

Only one thing is needed in a moment like that: to turn my attention to the One who loved me before I was born—before I did a single thing—and listen to what he has to say. There will be time later for the dishes, time later for the other chores of life. Time later for everything God wants me to accomplish. He'll let me know what else belongs on my list.

Jesus first. He is all I really need.

> *By wisdom a house is built,*
>   *and through understanding it is established;*
> *through knowledge its rooms are filled*
>   *with rare and beautiful treasures.*
>
> *Proverbs 24:3–4*

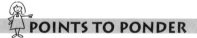

POINTS TO PONDER

1. Do you know any perfectionists? How has perfectionism (yours or someone else's) affected your life?

2. Who's your homemaking role model? What did you learn from that person? Make a list of the "shoulds" they taught you.

3. Today, what is your biggest challenge as a homemaker, career woman, wife, or mother (or all of the above!)? How do you manage?

Misguided Faith

I hesitated before knocking on Dorothy's apartment door. The last time I'd seen her I was five years old. Twenty years had passed. Would she remember me?

Dorothy and her husband, "Shooey," had been friends of my parents. We had lived in an identical brownstone apartment building next door to theirs, in an aging neighborhood just south of downtown Minneapolis near the heart of the city. Dorothy and Shooey, an older couple, had no children. As a child, I was often invited to visit, spending the afternoon with Dorothy while Shooey was at work.

On those afternoons, Dorothy let me sit at their big mahogany desk with its leather-trimmed desk blotter, drawing pictures with a gold pen on clean white stationery she kept in the top left desk drawer. When the mail arrived, I had the honor of retrieving it from the locked compartment in the building's lobby and then, back upstairs at the desk, slitting the envelopes open with a heavy brass letter opener, its carved ivory handle solid in my palm.

Dorothy even allowed me the incredible "honor" of carrying their trash from their apartment down the long, long hall to the incinerator access built into the wall. She'd hold the steel door open as I tossed the bag of garbage down the chute. She kept the door open so we could listen together for the satisfying plop as the trash landed far below, somewhere in the bowels of the building.

These were grown-up activities, privileges I never enjoyed at home. At home, my parents and we four children were packed into a tiny apartment. At home, chaos reigned and clean white paper was the stuff of dreams. At home, I was a mere serf; here I was a princess.

Late in the afternoon, Dorothy and I would sit together at the front window of the apartment, watching the traffic on the street below, waiting for Shooey to come home from work. I'd watch as he drove their green sedan into their garage across the street, one of a dozen garages in a long, low, wooden building. I'd watch Shooey emerge from the garage, lower the flat garage door, and stroll across the street, his black metal lunchbox swinging at his side. I'd listen for his steps on the landing, listen for the turn of the door latch, wait for him to open the apartment door. He always ducked entering the apartment, as tall men will do. I'd look up at him with my round face and he'd smile down at me. "Well, look who's here!" he'd say, feigning surprise. "It's Pie Face!" I'd hug his legs. He'd pat my head.

I loved him.

Later, we'd eat dinner, the three of us, at a polished, scratch-free drop-leaf table in a corner of the living room. We dined in elegance, with beautiful dishes, real silver utensils, and cloth napkins. I learned my best manners at that table.

Meanwhile, I knew, at home in that cramped basement apartment, my father, mother, brothers, and sister would be crowded around the old chrome and Formica table in our tiny kitchen, eating off Melmac plates with the stainless steel tableware my mother collected as premiums from boxes of laundry detergent. Poor peasants.

Dorothy and Shooey had a regal air of quiet nobility, but it was tinged with sadness. They were childless in the postwar baby boom. Friends (my parents, for instance) were teeming with offspring. Was that the source of their pain—the need to borrow children?

One Sunday morning, Dorothy invited me to church. Church was foreign to me; my parents slept in on Sundays. So did Shooey. I'd seen Dorothy walking alone on Sunday mornings, a queen in her elegant dresses, high heels, seamed stockings, and little fox stole. (The fox heads were still attached. Dorothy let me pet their tiny skulls with my fingertips, just once. The lifeless plastic eyes staring blankly gave me the creeps.)

It was a beautiful spring morning, the air cool and fresh from an overnight rainstorm. We walked together, her gloved hand warm on mine, the fox heads bouncing gently against Dorothy's bosom as she walked. What a privilege I'd been extended, to accompany her majesty on this glorious May day.

On the corner of East Seventeenth Street and First Avenue, I jumped ahead of her, off the curb, and into a large puddle in the gutter. Cold, muddy water splashed back onto Dorothy's legs and her beautiful dress. She let out a yelp, swinging the foxes out of harm's way. She began to scold me as she fumbled in her handbag for her white embroidered handkerchief. She continued to scold me as she sopped the glops from her stockings and skirt. She was silent as stone as we turned back toward home. There would be no church that morning. Dorothy never invited me to church again.

I wanted to die. I was five years old and I had failed. I had disappointed Dorothy. In an instant, I understood. The mud splatter was enough to banish me from the kingdom. I was imperfect. Too imperfect for Dorothy, for church, and for God.

God was the angry grown-up staring down at me as I stood in the puddle. My shoes and socks were soaking wet, soggy testimony to my guilt. I had nowhere to hide, no excuses, no way to lie my way out. I was guilty. Caught in the act. I willed the street to open up and swallow me whole. Oh, to have disappeared and not have to deal with this anger, not have to live with this disappointment—God's, Dorothy's, and my own. I was not perfect. And I was ashamed.

I was a five-year-old with no sense whatsoever. I couldn't see past the puddle to the mud splattering; I couldn't anticipate how it would ruin a proud queen's pretense and shatter her illusions that morning. I had no sense or sensibility, no control over my impulses, just a vast sweeping desire to kerplop into the water, mindless of even the possibility of the act having consequences.

So I jumped.

TO BE REMEMBERED

The memories rushed back as I stood in the hall of the brownstone, inhaling the familiar smell of dust and stale cigars. We moved away when I was five, to the other end of the city. Two decades had passed and the same wallpaper, now faded and more water-stained, hung on the walls above the mahogany wainscoting. The carpet had worn thinner and the hallway was much, much smaller than I remembered. The incinerator access was just a few feet beyond Dorothy's door, not nearly the epic journey it once was.

I knocked. Would she recognize me? I knocked again. The door opened and an aging queen—faded but still elegant—looked out at me. I glanced past her into the apartment. Nothing had changed. The television, the desk, the drop-leaf table were all in the same places. Dorothy remained here, trapped in time. Shooey, I'd heard from family friends, had passed on. I'd heard that Dorothy would be moving to Arizona soon to live with her niece. Another borrowed daughter.

"Pie Face!" she said as she smiled and swung the door wide.

LEARNING TO TRUST

I am still the pie-faced five-year-old with no sense whatsoever. I am still the fool, the child who followed birds down the sidewalk trying to sprinkle salt on their tails. An older neighbor boy, a boy I trusted, told me I could catch the birds that way. I tried and tried, with no results of course, and all the while becoming slowly aware that the boy was watching me from his window, laughing.

Misguided faith gets us into trouble. Misguided faith leads us into false notions about God, conclusions we draw based on relationships with imperfect people.

We think God is watching from the window, laughing as we make fools of ourselves. We hear God scolding us, shaming us, when we don't know any better than to do the foolish things we do. We imagine him banishing us from the kingdom, declaring us beyond redemption, hopelessly lost. We see him unwilling to forgive us, and it renders us unable to forgive ourselves. We imagine he is as petty, cold, ruthless, selfish, mean, and intolerant as we, or others we encounter, are. We are misguided.

And we are dead wrong.

We love. We trust. We lose. We grieve. The faith that will carry us through is certainly not the faith we put in those around us. "Do not put your trust in princes, in mortal men, who cannot save," says Psalm 146:3. The faith that will carry us through is not the belief we have in ourselves, in our ability to keep it all together. The faith we need is not found in positive affirmations, or an optimistic attitude, or in any success ethic or self-improvement program.

The faith we need is faith in the one true God, the One who alone is perfect, unchanging, and worthy of our trust. The laughter I heard as I shook salt at birds was not God's. Nor was it his voice scolding me for being a five-year-old unable to resist the pull of the puddle on a warm Sunday morning in spring. I'm certain Jesus himself found puddles irresistible when he was five. He knows. He knows.

When I listen carefully, prayerfully, I hear God's voice, full of compassion and full of forgiveness. Forgiving my ignorance, my misplaced faith. Forgiving as I confess the sins I willfully commit. Forgiving what I do in ignorance, sins I confess as I become aware.

When I listen closely, it's his voice I hear, conferring on me unmerited favor, declaring me his child, his heir, and a true daughter of the King of Kings—a real princess—forever.

Yet to all who received him, to those who believed in his name, he gave the right to become children of God.

John 1:12

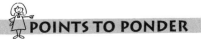

POINTS TO PONDER

1. Have you ever known someone like Dorothy? Describe her and your relationship with her.

2. What is your earliest memory of church? Of God?

3. Where do you stand today in matters of faith?

Holy Hormones!

CHAPTER TWELVE

I first heard about hormones in fifth grade, when the girls were invited to stay after school to watch "THE movie." The playground buzz said this movie was about "girl stuff like having babies and junk." Boys were not allowed to watch the movie, though a couple of infamous boys on the school audio-visual team were rumored to have seen parts of it. (This was back in the days when girls were unable to run movie projectors, repair cars, or work with wood and metal.)

The movie, produced by a leading manufacturer of feminine hygiene products, talked about menstruation, a subject of intense interest to young females. The shroud of secrecy meant this subject was taboo; we suspected it might even be a little "dirty." Nice girls didn't discuss such things in polite conversation.

So, of course, it was our favorite topic. "Have you started yet?" was the question of the hour. In fifth grade, a girl named Frances started during school. After a hushed conference with the teacher, Frances ran from our classroom to the girls' lavatory, flustered, the telltale red blotch on the back of her skirt betraying her awful secret. By the miracle of the grade school grapevine, everyone knew by recess. Poor Frances.

"How horrible," we said on the playground. "I'd just die if that happened to me." Years later, we still remembered Frances-Who-Started-in-School. I don't have a clue what her last name really was. No wonder women called it "The Curse."

Claiming to have The Curse was the only way to get out of swimming class in junior high. In this case, The Curse was a blessing. The gym teacher raised a skeptical eyebrow when a girl named Alice claimed to have The Curse four weeks in a row. Alice confided to the rest of us that she just didn't like wearing the shapeless red knit bathing suits the school forced on us. Well, who did? At that painfully self-conscious age, we were forced to parade around in bathing suits that left nothing to the imagination. This was embarrassing for those of us who only had imagination and little else. For our more buxom early-developing sisters, the embarrassment was far more acute. The suits offered nothing in the way of support or coverage. The rumor that the boys' locker room had a peephole into the pool area only added to our mortification.

The Curse was a handy excuse. We used it as often as we dared. By the early 1970s, our vocabulary had expanded. We had new code words for the monthly event. "Aunt Sally's come to town." "Grandma's here." "My little friend is visiting." But Ida still called it "The Curse."

Ida was a dignified woman in her fifties. One summer while I was in college, I worked in an office with Ida and a tall, twenty-something Swedish beauty named Sonja. Our boss, Mr. Johnson, was a middle-aged man. Sonja and I loved to tease Ida for her old-fashioned notions about The Curse. Modern girls like us were more open about the whole subject, we told her. It might have been the seventies, but Ida wasn't the least bit groovy.

One day Sonja noticed a magazine ad for feminine hygiene products picturing two exhausted Victorian women doing laundry with a washboard and a washtub. One of them scrubbed strips of white cloth in the tub while the other hung them on a clothesline to dry. The caption read, "No wonder they called it 'The Curse.'" Sonja clipped the page from the magazine and slid it under the glass on top of Ida's desk while Ida was out to lunch. We waited.

Ida came in, crossing the office to her desk. We watched her glance down. She spotted the ad. Her eyebrows came together as she studied it, and then arched up as a flicker of understanding crossed her face. She drew in a sharp breath. Her cheeks flushed. In a flash, she lifted the glass with one hand and swished the page out with the other, opened her top desk drawer, and stuffed the paper away. Beet-faced, she glared at us and hissed, "What if Mr. Johnson had seen that?"

Sonja and I laughed harder. "Oh, horrors!" Sonja said through tears. "He probably doesn't know about The Curse!"

It took Ida a week before she could laugh with us. She probably called it The Curse until the day she died. I'll bet Frances in fifth grade called it that, too.

THE CURSE CONTINUES

My hormones have been a curse for years. I was in denial for the longest time, thinking my hormones were under control. I refused to see how my moods affected my relationships with my husband, my children, my friends, and my coworkers.

The truth is, there are certain times when good communication with me is impossible, when everything my husband, Terry, says rubs me the wrong way. He says, "The scrambled eggs are really good this morning."

I say, "What was wrong with the eggs I made the other day?"

He says, "You look nice today."

"And I looked awful yesterday?"

Hormones are an invisible force of destruction. A trap for the unsuspecting husband who casually brings up a subject he thinks can't possibly be incendiary—mowing the lawn, for instance—and it blows up in his face.

"Looks like the lawn needs mowing," he says offhandedly.

I burst into tears, sobbing, "I'm a failure as a homemaker! I try to keep up with everything but just can't seem to please you. I don't know why you even married me, miserable wretch that I am. Besides that, I'm FAT!"

Or it could go in another direction. "Looks like the lawn needs mowing," he says casually. I lay into him like a mixer in meringue.

"Oh sure! I guess I'm supposed to take care of THAT, TOO? I don't suppose there is any chance that maybe YOU could take time away from YOUR precious schedule to get that little job done, IS THERE? Probably NOT! I'm sure you have something IMPORTANT to do on Saturday, like SLEEPING! Well, FINE! I'll just see what I can do about that, along with everything ELSE I have to do around here!"

"Where did THAT come from?" he says, mouth agape.

I burst into tears. "I don't know! Just hold me." He looks at me like I've just invited him to kiss a porcupine.

"Not with all those quills in the way," he says.

I realized how often my hormones affected our relationship one morning as I drove to work. I had had a fight with Terry that morning over something completely stupid, and as I drove, I thought, *Why in the world did I ever marry that guy? What did I ever see in him?*

On the radio, a woman doctor described her own experience with PMS. She said she knew she was PMSing when she would suddenly, for no reason whatsoever, start thinking her husband was a complete jerk. She'd ask herself, *Why did I ever marry this guy?*

I nearly drove into a light pole. I realized I had been thinking that about Terry on a regular monthly basis! I had to admit it. I was a hormone hostage.

Some hormonally charged days, it would be nice if I had something like a car alarm on me, so when Terry ventures too close it would say, "WARNING! STEP AWAY FROM THE WOMAN!" He says my hormones are the reason we've never kept guns in the house.

Now as I plunge toward menopause, a nagging thought plagues me. *What if, after all those years of blaming my nasty moods on my hormones, I go through menopause and discover I just had a really rotten personality all along?*

MENOPAUSE MOMENTS

This is the story of a woman who, on her fifty-first birthday, feels rotten. *I must be heading toward menopause,* she thinks. *I just want to scream at everyone, "LEAVE ME ALONE!"* She worries that she'll start screaming and screaming such things and not be able to stop. She's even been tempted to swear. This worries her.

She knows her family would be appalled, especially her husband. Whenever she says anything raw and honest, he wrinkles up his nose and says, "Oh, you don't mean that." She thinks, *Yes, I do mean it! Why else would I say it?* She thinks that, but she says, "You're right, dear. I'm sorry I said that. I should not have said that." The truth is she isn't the least bit sorry, and she's never meant anything more firmly in her life.

The woman is tired, so very tired, of saying she is sorry when she is not. *Why can't I say what I want to say?* she wonders. *I'm over fifty. What is my problem? I'm not old enough to say what I want?*

"The whole world can just lump it if they don't like it," she says to the woman in the mirror who looks very much like her mother. *How did this happen? When did my stomach start to pooch out like that? When did my shoulders get so rounded?*

"You have such beautiful posture," her mother used to tell her. She'd stand up taller and straighter. Now it feels like so much work to straighten up. *Am I getting osteoporosis?* she wonders. *Thank goodness, they don't call it "dowager's hump" anymore. Osteoporosis sounds better.*

She'd had a bone scan earlier, a couple years ago at a women's conference. Two young nurses did the test.

"You're losing bone density," they told her.

"How can that be?" she said. "I exercise. I eat calcium-rich foods. I take supplements. I don't smoke or drink. How is this possible? How can I be losing density?"

The bouncy young girls with the thick, thick bones just smiled and shrugged. "We don't know," they confessed. "Sometimes, it's just genetic. Are you descended from northern Europeans?"

She wanted to scream at them, "What do you two know about getting older? What do you know about drying up and feeling useless?" She wanted to scream that, but she didn't. She imagined how they'd wrinkle up their noses and whisper, "Crazy old woman," as she walked away. So, she swallowed the urge to scream, snatched the computer printout of her feeble bones from the young girl's hand, and walked to the snack counter.

Maybe it's the caffeine, she thought, ordering a large diet Coke. *Maybe it's genetics. Maybe it's a losing battle. Maybe I'm just a lost cause. Do all women feel this way at one time or another?*

The following week, she's having a latté with her friend Louise, a woman about her same age, at the local coffee house. Louise confides over a cup of Tanzanian Teaberry Decaf, "I just don't know what is wrong with me. I'm mad all the time. I'm mad at Jack, mad at the kids. I'm just mad. All the time."

"You're ticked off," the woman says. "You're getting older and it just ticks you off."

"Yes! That's it," Louise says, surprised. "I'm just ... um ... just ticked off."

They drink coffee in silence for a minute. The woman wants to ask her friend if she ever feels like screaming, or even swearing, but she's afraid Louise, who had trouble saying "ticked off," will wrinkle up her nose in disgust at the thought of such a public display.

The woman thinks about her own grandfather, a fine church-going citizen who said, when he was upset, "Oh goodness!" If he was really perturbed, he said, "Oh goodness, goodness!" It was as close as he ever came to using profanity. What would he think if she ran around screaming and swearing? Oh goodness, goodness.

The silence is broken when Louise asks, "Are you eating tofu these days? Soy is supposed to be good for what ails us." She blathers on and on about tofu this and soy that. The woman thinks, *Blah, blah, blah. Soy schmoy. Who cares about tofu? I'm too tired to care anymore. I don't care about soy, or density, or anything. It's just too much work to care.*

She wants to run from the café screaming and swearing like a crazy sailor, Grandpa be darned. But she imagines the whole world wrinkling its nose at her. The woman orders another latté instead, while her friend chatters on about HRT versus phytoestrogens and the benefits of acupuncture in treating hot flashes.

Louise says, "I've heard aroma therapy with massage feels wonderful." The woman slurps the whipped cream—extra calcium—from the top of her latté and tries to remember what wonderful felt like.

HEARD IT THROUGH THE GRAPEVINE

We learned about "female things" from The Movie or The Booklet, from our older sisters, our mothers, our aunts, our cousins, and our friends. Such information has passed along the female information highway for eons. I imagine the women in the Bible, passing information from one generation to the next around the town well. I imagine pioneer women talking about these things on the wagon trains, in their houses of sod, and in their cabins. I remember the women in the old neighborhoods of the city where I grew up, talking over the back fence, talking on the street, on their front porches, and on the benches in the park.

I remember my aunts visiting my mother, talking at the kitchen table over coffee. I listened from the other room; children were not allowed to sit in on such discussions. I heard about Harriet's hemorrhages ("Six pads an hour before she could get to the hospital . . ."), and Margaret's long labor ("Forty-six hours of agony! She swears Junior will be an only child . . ."). Forty-six hours of pain? Hearing that, I vowed to remain childless, though Margaret had five more babies after Junior. She was my inspiration the first time I was in labor, as I chanted, "If it was so bad, Junior would still be an only child . . ."

I heard about my aunt's neighbor's friend, a woman in her forties who had been childless. She went to the doctor thinking she had a tumor and discovered she was seven months pregnant. "For the first two years of the baby's life, she called her 'my little tumor'!"

I listened to the funny stories, the dramatic legends of womanly suffering, and the tales of family sorrow. I heard about the two babies my father's family lost in an epidemic of diphtheria in the early 1900s. I heard about my maternal grandmother's last baby—number eleven—who was stillborn.

Listening to those stories, I learned what it meant to be female, that our gender carried a mysterious and scary curse of pain and heartbreak through life. And it has been ever thus. Eve made a lousy choice. The curse of painful childbirth is her legacy. And the Old Testament message of "uncleanness" can make a woman feel "cursed" indeed. If the story stopped there, a girl could get downright depressed about being a girl.

But Jesus says we are more than our bodies, more than our body functions. In Christ, we have purpose and ministry, and it continues as we age. The New Testament gives us "older women" a clear directive in Titus 2:3–5. We have a job to do: teaching and encouraging younger women. And women have been operating under this instruction for generations.

A Titus woman in nurse's garb held my hand during labor. Titus women are across the table in the coffee house, in the grocery aisles, or in the house next door, offering encouragement and sharing wisdom.

"Hang in there. Toddlers eventually grow out of this . . ."

"Children recover from these things. You'll be amazed. You won't even notice the scar . . ."

"Don't give up. Keep loving and keep praying. Fourteen is a tough age . . ."

It's our mandate. It's our ministry. It's our purpose. In the hardest of times, the Titus woman comes alongside to say, "You are so blessed to have this child. He's a gift. You can do this . . ."

She says, "Your mother was a wonderful woman. We'll all miss her . . ."

In the darkest moment, she is there, holding your hand and whispering, "Trust God. He has a plan for your life, even now ... Even with this ..."

> *Every good and perfect gift is from above, coming*
> *down from the Father of the heavenly lights,*
> *who does not change like shifting shadows.*
>
> *James 1:17*

POINTS TO PONDER

1. How did you learn the facts of life? What advice or information did you pick up from the grapevine as you were growing up?

2. Describe your most embarrassing adolescent moment.

3. What advice would you give to a twelve-year-old girl today?

Mentalpause

I called American Express last week to fix an error on our bill. The customer service rep put me on hold while she made the correction. When she came back on the line, she said, "Thank you for waiting. This is what I did . . ." She paused for several long moments and then said, "Now what was it I did?" She laughed. I laughed.

"I understand," I said. "It's been such a long time since you did it."

She laughed again. "Yes, I'm having a senior moment . . ."

Just the other day, I started to tell my twenty-something daughter a story and she stopped me midsentence. "You already told me that story. Yesterday," she said. I was mortified. This was something *old* people did!

"It's okay, Mom," she said. "I understand. It's mentalpause."

Senior moments. Mentalpause. Old-timer's disease. I'm sick of hearing about those things. And I'm tired of all those Internet lists: "Fifty Ways to Know You're Over Fifty" and the "How

You Know You're Old" jokes. "My back goes out more often than I do." "I get winded playing video games." I'm sick of it all!

We're all getting older. Do we need to keep reminding each other? Oh sure, it's all funny, in a "misery loves company" sort of way. But enough is enough!

Maybe it's all just payback. I used to laugh at my mother for absentmindedly putting the milk in the cupboard and the salt-shaker in the refrigerator. Now I do the same things. Last week I misplaced the dog. She ran into the garage as I was unloading groceries. I locked her out there. Four hours later, Terry asked where she was. I looked at him blankly, thinking, *Do we have a dog?*

"Dog?" I said. "I don't know. She was here a minute ago, wasn't she?" I was sure I'd just seen her trot through the kitchen.

The other day I searched for my half-slip, digging through dresser drawers, rummaging through the hamper. It was nowhere to be found. I was wearing a heavy skirt, so I decided I'd just go without the slip. Before leaving the house, I stopped in the bathroom. As I was readjusting myself, I found the slip. Right there under my skirt. I'd been wearing it all along. Sad thing is, I'd already looked there once.

One morning last week, I chased our car down the driveway in my robe and slippers, waving and hollering at my departing husband. When I caught up to the car, he stopped and lowered the car window. I panted, "You'd better not leave without kissing me goodbye!"

"I'd be glad to kiss you again, but I just did. By the microwave. Five minutes ago."

This has nothing to do with his kissing. This has everything to do with my mind.

What is happening to my mind? My life has become a journalism exercise—answering the five W's and the H. *What was I just saying? Where did I leave the dog? When did we get a dog? Why did I come into this room? Why did I get down on my knees—to pray or to clean the dust from under the bed? Who is this woman in the mirror? When did she lose her grip? How did I get to this sorry state?*

"With age comes wisdom." That's a lie, at least in my case. The longer I live, the less I know, due to a combination of factors. One is "brain fog." Facts that once were clear and prominent are now hidden under a blanket of fog that's settled in the valleys between the ridges of my cerebral cortex. It's like any other fog bank: you know the ground is still there, but darned if you can see it anymore.

Then there's the harsh reality that I've murdered gazillions of brain cells watching reruns on Nick at Nite. (June Cleaver still wears her pearls with every single outfit, just in case you're curious and don't have cable.) Another gazillion brain cells have voluntarily leapt out my ears, in a desperate effort to save themselves from having to think my increasingly stupid thoughts. *Should I switch to Country Blossom air freshener or stick with Tahitian Spice? Should I wear the plaid top with the green skirt, or the red top with the blue skirt? Where is my half-slip?* These are the deep things I ponder. I hear my brain cells muttering as they pack their bags, "You'd think just ONCE she'd contemplate world peace or quantum physics, but noooo . . ."

So age has not brought wisdom. Between the brain cells jumping ship and the fog over the rest of the harbor, navigating the waters of life gets tougher by the day. The longer I live the less I know. (Did I tell you that already? Or can't you remember either?) But the good news is I'm less aware that I don't know it. (If that made sense to you, you are obviously younger than I am.)

I missed a meeting a few weeks back. A meeting I had called. A meeting other women had to arrange childcare to attend. A meeting I was supposed to be leading. I sat in my office that morning, thinking how nice it was to have some free time. I glanced at the clock. *9:30? Oh NO! I was supposed to be at that meeting at 8:00!*

I know what you're thinking. I should have reminded myself about the meeting. I did. I checked my calendar the night before and said to myself, "I have that meeting in the morning." And when I got up that morning, I had absolutely no thought of that meeting whatsoever.

That's why I got an electronic brain, one of those handheld marvels of artificial intelligence that holds everything: addresses, phone numbers, task lists, journals, notes, books, calculators, games, E-mail, calendars, and appointments. I'd never miss another meeting. I'd never miss another anything. This would be my brain.

It seems the brain has a mind of its own. Lights blink. Alarms go off. It makes noises I'd never make in public. All the information I need is available at the touch of a button. But which button? I know this thing is brilliant. I just can't speak its language. And what good does it do me if I forget to take it with me? How often can I use the excuse, "I'm sorry. I left my brain at home"?

I had a high-tech problem. I discovered a low-tech solution: the Sticky Note System. The humble sticky note is a lifesaver for the middle-aged. When I have an appointment, after writing it on my paper calendar and entering it in my electronic brain, I also write a reminder on several sticky notes. I stick one on the door leading out to the garage, another on the kitchen cupboard, a third on the bathroom mirror, and the last on my bedside lamp. This at least lowers the risk of missing another meeting.

The Sticky Note System is great, but not perfect. I keep a pad of stickies in the laundry room. On laundry day, I write "BUY SOAP" and stick the note to my shirt; later I stick it to the shopping list on the refrigerator. Unfortunately, by shopping day I'm wondering, BUY SOAP? *Was that dish, hand, dishwasher, bath, or dog soap?*

I keep sticky notes next to the TV so I can jot down good ideas from the "better living" channels. Later I look at the note stuck to the cupboard door and wonder, *Was this a recipe or instructions for homemade wallpaper paste?* I won't know until I taste it.

Sticky notes are handy in the car, too. "PICK UP DRY CLEANING" and "PICK UP HUSBAND" are good things to remember. (I chuckle at the irony as "GET GAS" flutters from the dashboard just as I pull into Taco Bob's drive-thru and order Bob's Bean Burrito Extremo Especiale, Extra Grande. *Check.*)

WHERE WAS I? OH, YEAH ...

Okay, so I'm losing it. The most encouraging research I've come across suggests that *mental* symptoms may be the first symptoms of the approaching "change of life." And these mental symptoms can start much earlier than you might think. In the forties. Even in the thirties! Yikes!

The list of possible mental symptoms is a long one. Reading the list, I thought, *Has this researcher been peeking in my windows?* "Bright" women *(if it happens to "bright" women what hope is there for the rest of us?)* reported the following symptoms: losing their train of thought, forgetting what they'd just read, missing meetings, and misplacing things. *(Dogs, perhaps?)* At times, they felt cotton-headed and experienced foggy thinking. *(Hmm.)* They feared repeating themselves, asking, "Did I tell you this already?" *(Ha!)*

They had momentary lapses where they blanked out on an ingrained skill, such as how to start the car. They found themselves unable to focus and easily distracted. *(I had to read that part three times. Did you?)* They drew blanks trying to remember the words to songs, why they came into a room, birthdays, and ATM codes. *(Or kissing someone maybe?)*

Angry and frustrated, these bright women worried about the early onset of Alzheimer's, got depressed, and lost sleep. They had crying spells, for no apparent reason. *(Gasp!)* They didn't want to admit these feelings, for fear of eroding their own credibility and undermining others' confidence in them. *(Yes! Yes!)* They wanted to just give up trying, give up competing, and put themselves out to pasture like an old racehorse. *(Sob!)*

Been there. Felt that.

The really good news? These bright women were normal. NORMAL! These cognitive symptoms were the early warning signals of the physical changes to come. This "perimenopause" was a normal hormone-related condition, just as pregnancy is a normal hormone-related condition.

Given the size of the Baby Boom bulge in the population, I realized that millions of women out there were going through the same things I was experiencing. We were all together in the "pause" before menopause. And we weren't "losing it." We were all just being normal!

I informed my family. "Please, no more remarks about mentalpause or senior moments. I am simply exhibiting the symptoms accompanying normal hormonal changes. So I would appreciate it if you would stop implying—however subtle you think twirling your index finger next to your temple might be—that I am nuts!"

The following week, I knew they'd gotten my message. I had another momentary brain fade while I was talking to my daughter on the phone, and she said, "Well, Mom, you sure are normal today!" *Yes!*

It does help to lighten up. Just the other day, my husband and I discussed something important, about which I recall nothing now. I just know it was important! I told him, "It's that other shoe thing . . ."

"What 'other shoe thing'?" he asked.

"I feel like I'm waiting for the other shoe," I said.

"For the other shoe to . . . ?" I knew he was trying to help, but darned if I could remember what the "other shoe" was supposed to do. I did the only thing I could do. I laughed.

"What's happening to me?" I wailed. "I'm losing it!"

"You're not the only one," he said. He looked around to make sure nobody else was listening. (We've been home alone for ages, but he still checks for "little pitchers.") He continued.

"Remember the other night you asked me to pick up milk on the way home? Well, I pulled into the garage and thought, *Oh, NO! I forgot the milk.* I reached into the back seat for my briefcase and there on the floor in back were two gallons of milk. I hadn't forgotten to get it. I just forgot to remember that I got it!" I was glad the children weren't home to hear this.

Meanwhile, I'll rely on paper planners, my electronic brain, and the Sticky Note System. All of which will soon be obsolete, because medical science keeps promising to fix my brain. Each time I see an article about procedures or products that promise to reverse the effects of aging on the brain, hope flares briefly. *Can they do that? What if I am too far gone? What if my synapses are so soggy they can no longer fire?* (My three remaining brain cells are packing at this point. I can feel it. I realize I'm hopeless. You have to give science something to work with.)

HOW IT IS, HOW IT WILL BE

"The Lord giveth . . ." and time taketh some of it away. That's just how it is. But omniscience has always been God's domain, not ours. What matters most, I see now, are not the brilliant flashes of insight I've had, but the quiet understandings I've come to.

It may take me twice as long now to think of half as much, but I'm not in such a hurry anymore. I enjoy taking extra time now to linger in God's love. "Abide with me," Jesus says. I long to rest in his fellowship, to know deeper peace in his presence. And the Holy Spirit is forever there, as promised in John 14:26, to help me remember what I've learned.

It may take me longer to put a name to a familiar face I see, but the day is coming when I will no longer "see but a poor reflection as in a mirror; then we shall see face to face. Now I know in part; then I shall know fully, even as I am fully known" (1 Corinthians 13:12).

I will know Jesus when I see him, and as he promised, on that glorious day he will remember me.

> *Who has known the mind of the Lord that he may*
> *instruct him?*
> *But we have the mind of Christ.*
>
> *1 Corinthians 2:16*

POINTS TO PONDER

1. Umm . . . what was this chapter about again?

2. What have you forgotten lately?

3. If you can remember, describe any "memory aids" you've used. What's helped you most in keeping track of the details of your life?

What? Me Botox?

CHAPTER FOURTEEN

It all started back in 1987, when a dermatologist noticed his receptionist frowned deeper and deeper as the day wore on. He suggested a little shot of something called Botox between the eyebrows to paralyze those frown muscles. The results were great. A win-win situation: she had no more frown lines, and the doctor didn't have to worry about improving his receptionist's working conditions. The Botox Revolution was born.

The Botox Party is the latest home party fad as I write this. The hostess invites her friends and a doctor brings the Botox. Between the bean dip and the crab rolls, partygoers take turns getting the injections. Hard to believe, isn't it? But it's true!

By the time I got wind of it, Botox had been the rage in Europe and on both American coasts for ages. I wasn't surprised I'd never heard of it. Women here in America's "flyover zone" are not usually the first to pick up on the latest trends. Women in the Australian outback might be a little less current than we are, but not much.

When I first heard the word *Botox,* I figured it must have something to do with cows. "Bo" usually means "bovine" in these parts, and one woman did describe her newly Botoxed forehead as "smooth as a new calfskin wallet." But the *bo* comes from the bacteria that causes botulism. That's food poisoning, which explains the *tox* part.

Botulinum toxin or Botox had long been used to treat facial tics and other serious facial muscular disorders. Then it was approved by the FDA for use in treating other critical situations—like crow's-feet and frown lines.

"Let me see if I understand this whole deal," my husband said when I told him about Botox. "Women are willing to pay five or six hundred dollars every few months to have a needle full of poison injected into their face. Why?"

"So they won't look like they're frowning," I said, demonstrating with a furrowed brow. "Ridiculous, isn't it?" He didn't answer. He just stared at my forehead, probably thinking "no more frowning" might be a good thing in a wife.

All that money, and the effect doesn't even last. It's like Cinderella at midnight. Suddenly the Botox wears off and her face falls back into its pre-injection state. The other irony is that Botox works best, the experts say, in younger, thinner skin. Like those people need it!

Newsweek magazine covered the Botox boom, predicting that the once feared poison could mean billions of dollars for cosmetic surgeons—billions paid by women afraid of aging. It promised to be the Boomers' miracle drug. The article raised the question "Is it safe?" and the bigger question, "Why are we so vain?"

As I read that, I heard Carly Simon's old song, "You're So Vain," in my head. Carly was right. The song is about us. We think everything is about us.

Botox works by paralyzing muscles, a temporary effect that wears off in a few months. Mistakes happen. A misdirected shot to the eyebrows can leave you looking perpetually surprised. (Don't parents of college students look that way automatically?)

A poorly aimed dose near the mouth may give you a permanent smile. I had the same look as my daughter introduced me to one of her boyfriends—a lad with spiked orange hair and a brass nose ring connected to his earlobe by a length of doggy choke chain.

The permanent smile can help when your adult child appears on your doorstep, bags in hand, asking to move back in and live rent-free, "just until I get back on my feet." You want to scream, but thanks to Botox, you just smile serenely, as you remember how long it took them to find those feet and use them to walk out the door in the first place. You continue to smile as you deliver the bad news. "Sorry, dear. We're moving to . . . uh . . . Bethlehem. There's no room at the inn."

A shot gone wrong near the lips left one woman drooling, unable to whistle, drink through a straw, or talk coherently for a month. Every parent of a teenager knows that feeling. You are talking to the child (okay, maybe lecturing) about something important. He stares at you without expression.

"Got that?" you ask.

"Wha'?" he says.

"Is my mouth not working?" you ask. You might as well be trying to whistle through drool. Botox mistakes last only a few weeks. The side effects of having children last much longer.

I was amazed to read about generations of women taking the injections together—the latest in mother-daughter bonding, I guess. Remember the commercials for the dish-washing liquid that kept your hands looking young? Looking at the hands of two women, you had to guess which hands were the mother's and which were the daughter's. Imagine the Botox commercials. "Which face is the daughter's, which is the mother's? Now which is the grandmother's?" It will be a tough call. All three will have the same permanently surprised look.

One woman said she started using Botox because she looked tired and unhappy. Perhaps that's because she *was* tired and unhappy. Had she tried the revolutionary remedy of a good night's sleep? Can "unhappy" be cured by a shot of poison in the forehead?

What is so bad about letting your feelings show on your face? God designed the face as a key communication tool. How will a Botoxed mother control her children in church if she can't glower at them? How will Botoxed teachers keep their classes in line if they can't give them "the eye"?

Botox use is so common in the movie and television industry these days directors are getting frustrated. What good is an actress if her face can't show emotion? Imagine Garbo's famous line, "I vant to be alone," delivered with her eyebrows frozen in surprise. *I vant to be alone? I do?*

And Botox would have ruined the scene where Bacall told Bogie, "You do know how to whistle, don't you, Steve? You just put your lips together and blow . . ." *You can put your lips together, can't you? Try not to drool! Wipe that silly grin off your face! What is your PROBLEM?*

Botox proponents—the profiteers—are making a fortune on our fears. Why are we so afraid of getting older? Why are we so afraid to show our age? Why do we think we must be "forever young"?

Botox may have no long-term negative physical effects, but what of the mental effects? The "look young" mentality paralyzes the mind. We stop thinking rationally and start believing that aging gracefully is not nearly as important as looking good at any age. We are in deep denial of the fact that our days on this earth are numbered. We cling to the illusion that we will live forever, and now the illusion, thanks to Botox and cosmetic surgery, that we will live forever young.

What we need is a Botox shot to the part of our brain that thought all this was a good idea.

WAKING UP THE SISTERHOOD

I've only agreed with Gloria Steinem two times since 1972. This is one of them. She is all in favor of wrinkles. So am I. All this Botox business flies in the face of women's struggle to be valued less for how we look and more for how we think. If Gloria calls a protest, I'll be right there marching in the front line shouting, "Wake up, sisters! We've come a long way, baby! Let's not go back! Liberate your thinking. Burn your Botox party invitation. Wear your wrinkles proudly. You've earned them!"

Can't we accept our wrinkles as honorable? Can't we carry them proudly as mementos of a life well-lived? When do we stop thinking so much about how we look and think more about how we are living? When will we worry less about our outsides and be more concerned with the inner qualities of grace, patience, kindness, and forgiveness?

Do I look at my sweet, old mother's wrinkled face and cringe? Of course not! She has earned every one of her wrinkles; some of them were gifts from me. My own "bunny lines" across the bridge of my nose came from crinkling my nose in disgust. Disgust is often a passionate reaction to things in life. Reacting is part of being alive. My crow's-feet have deepened with the years of smiling and laughing. I wouldn't trade them for anything.

My frown lines are a sign that I care deeply—more deeply year by year if the lines are a true measure. Pain affects me. Imagine listening to a friend's horror story of divorce or her cancer battle, and not being able to frown. I don't want to tell my troubles to someone whose face has been smoothed into a plastic mask. I can get that reaction talking to a Barbie doll.

Human facial expression is part of God's design, allowing us to communicate surprise, compassion, fear, love, or delight. When did it become so awful to look like we are angry or sad or tired or (heaven forbid) old? "There is a time for everything . . . under heaven," the Bible says, "a time to weep and a time to laugh, a time to mourn and a time to dance" (Ecclesiastes 3:1, 4). A time to smile, a time to laugh, a time to be angry, and a time to frown.

I don't want my brows frozen in a look of permanent surprise. I don't want the skin of my forehead taut as new leather. I don't want a perpetual smile. I want the years I've survived to show.

Life goes on, and as we grow older we hopefully understand more of God's perspective, the bigger picture of living. "The LORD does not look at the things man looks at. Man looks at the outward appearance, but the LORD looks at the heart" (1 Samuel 16:7). We too can look beyond the physical and look at the heart, at the character—our own and others'. As we learn to accept ourselves, we can accept others. We learn to forgive. We learn to cherish. We learn to live.

And our faces show it.

> *There is a time for everything,*
> *and a season for every activity under heaven:*
> *a time to be born and a time to die,*
> *a time to plant and a time to uproot,*
> *a time to kill and a time to heal,*
> *a time to tear down and a time to build,*
> *a time to weep and a time to laugh,*
> *a time to mourn and a time to dance,*
> *a time to scatter stones and a time to gather them,*
> *a time to embrace and a time to refrain,*
> *a time to search and a time to give up,*
> *a time to keep and a time to throw away,*
> *a time to tear and a time to mend,*

a time to be silent and a time to speak,

a time to love and a time to hate,

a time for war and a time for peace.

Ecclesiastes 3:1–8

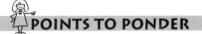
POINTS TO PONDER

1. What do you think about using something like Botox or having cosmetic surgery to look younger? Would you? Have you ever? Why or why not?

2. "You can never be too rich or too thin," we've been told. What do you think of the barrage of messages aimed at making us feel we are not good enough as we are? What impact has this culture had on you and other women you know?

3. What does it mean to "age gracefully"? Are you?

What Price Beauty?

CHAPTER FIFTEEN

My mother felt ugly her whole life. I remember her saying it, again and again, like a mantra. She believed it. I was shocked that she would think it.

Mother stood at the bathroom mirror putting on her makeup for an evening out. I was young, perhaps nine or ten, and I sat on the toilet lid, watching, fascinated, as she stroked mascara onto her lashes with a little brush. My mother didn't go out often in the evenings. She was an at-home mother. Makeup was reserved for special occasions.

She'd applied her foundation, then the mascara. She rubbed pink rouge onto each cheek, and then opened her mouth, lips taut. She drew a cupid's bow with lipstick on her upper lip, filled in the sides with red, then smoothed the color across her lower lip twice. She reached for a square of toilet tissue to blot her lips.

As she leaned near me, I smelled her perfume and told her she was pretty. She smiled at me, an indulgent mother's smile, as if I didn't know what I was talking about.

Decades later, my mother and I are looking at an old photograph. In the picture, Mother stands outdoors in front of a blooming lilac bush. She is thirteen years old. The original black and white photo has been colored by a photo artist, as was the fashion years ago. My mother's cheeks are tinted pink, her dress a pale blue, and the lilacs a soft lavender. Her round face is open, her smile shy, and she radiates good health and sweetness of spirit.

My mother stands straight and tall, her left arm draped around the shoulders of Fay, her childhood friend. Fay, shorter and darker, has thick dark hair and one of those faces that hints at a more mature, future beauty. She stands with one hand on her hip, and the hip pushed out. Fay is sassy. Confident.

I hold the picture toward my mother. "I love this picture," I say, loving the girl my mother used to be, admiring the strong, fine figure she cut.

"I was so ugly," my mother says, "especially next to Fay. She was the pretty one. Always the pretty one."

"All teenagers feel that way, don't they?"

"I felt ugly my whole life," she says again. "Ugly. Awkward. Gawky. My whole life."

"I was always so proud when you came to my school. You were the prettiest mother in the class!"

"Well, I always felt ugly," she says.

There are certainly virtues that transcend the physical, virtues my mother possesses in abundance. Hardworking, reliable, and practical, she was a good, sturdy girl who grew up to be a good, sturdy woman. She is also beautiful, and I tell her so.

"Beautiful. Ha! Nobody ever accused me of that," she laughs. "Except your father, and what did he know? He was in love, and love is blind!"

My mother felt ugly her whole life. All through my impressionable years she'd said it, reinforcing a clear message: Beautiful is better. Some of us have it; some don't. With that message came another, subtler message: Ugly begets ugly. If my mother was ugly, I must be ugly, too. My only hope was that love, the blind kind, would also find me one day.

THE FEMININE IDEAL

When do such notions begin to wedge themselves into our psyche? For my fifth birthday, I had a cake with a doll standing in the middle of a beautiful frosted cake skirt. Barbie had not been invented yet, so this must have been her older sister. Much has been made of the negative influence Barbie and her ilk have had on our culture. The ideal of impossible physical perfection has stoked the fires of self-loathing in females around the globe for ages, but it didn't start with Barbie.

The doll in the middle of my cake was every bit as impossibly beautiful as Barbie would be later. That doll was the embodiment of all my little girl dreams—dreams of becoming a beauty, a princess, a gorgeous creature in a long frosted skirt, my long hair piled high on my head. Regal in my huge, glorious gown, I'd be the envy of every girl at the party. Barbie didn't start our fairy-tale dreaming. Mass marketers just capitalized on the movie already playing in our heads, inspired by the fairy-tale femmes fatales.

Cinderella turned from a practical, hardworking, dowdy girl into a beauty. The ugly stepsisters got zip. Sleeping Beauty—not Sleeping Ugly, not Sleeping Great Personality, but Sleeping Beauty—was the one who awakened to the kiss of her prince. Rapunzel's beautiful hair attracted her handsome savior. Even the Ugly Duckling found the redemption of beauty, transformed by time into a gorgeous swan. The message was clear. Mother was right. Beautiful is better. Beauty gets the prince, the party, and the prize.

But let's not blame it all on the Brothers Grimm and Hans Christian Andersen. Wasn't the biblical Esther the "fairest of them all"? Didn't humble Ruth win the heart of Boaz with her inner and outer beauty in a real "Cinderella" story? Delilah and Bathsheba had their faults, but they were both "lookers."

Tales of the power of beauty, and the power of beautiful women, are as old as time. Maybe it's desire for that power driving some mothers to dress their little girls up like mini-Dolly Partons and parade them across the stage in "kiddy queen" pageants. Maybe these mothers don't see that all little girls are absolute beauties, that they are already adorable little princesses, already winners. Maybe these mothers are sating their own unfulfilled desires. Maybe their heads are filled with a twist on "ugly begets ugly": If ugly can beget beauty, maybe ugly wasn't so ugly after all.

What happens to the losers in those contests, to all the girls like my mother and me? What happens to the rest of us in a culture that lauds beauty at all cost, that holds up images of impossibly beautiful women and dares us to compete? Is it any wonder we begin to compare ourselves to other women?

Their hair shimmers and bounces; ours is dull and limp. Their teeth are straighter, whiter, and gap-free. Their lips are more luscious than ours and their lipstick lasts all day. We haven't had thighs as small and smooth as theirs since grade school. Even their behinds are ahead of ours.

Let's face it. We lose. "The pretty one" always wins. The message the culture gives us is soon so ingrained it sounds like original thought. We feel awful about ourselves. We feel ugly.

Test this yourself. Go to your local clothing store. Stand in front of the dressing room mirror in your unmentionables and try saying, "I look good just the way I am. I look great without losing any weight. My behind is just fine the way it is."

Who can say such things under the fluorescent lights before the full-length mirror? Only the bravest among us. You might say it, but you'll have trouble convincing the woman in the mirror that it's true. Can you appreciate the irony that the woman in the dressing room next door, that little slip of a girl who just ducked in there with six bikinis and four pairs of short shorts, is thinking the same thing you are? *I look horrible. I have to lose some weight. What is going on with my behind?*

DRAWING THE LINE

Where do we draw the line? I've seen several television shows lately documenting cases of cosmetic surgery gone wrong. Women seeking beauty through surgery were left disfigured, misshapen, and scarred. In every case, their "before" pictures looked fine. I saw absolutely nothing wrong with the way they looked. *It has to be pure vanity,* I thought.

Is there no end to their pathetic pursuit of perfection? Have they no limits on their Visa cards?

I judged them harshly, until I noticed that a mole on my face was growing larger. From a health perspective, I could justify the mole's removal, since moles can be cancerous and lead to all sorts of scary problems. My doctor recommended I see the cosmetic surgeon down the hall. She said, "I don't want to take any chances with your face." (God had. Why couldn't she?)

At the cosmetic surgeon's office, I decided that, as long as he was right there removing one mole he might as well take off another one growing near my eyelid. And two more near my hairline. Nobody ever saw those, but as long as he was there . . . Ten minutes and a whiff of singed eyebrow later, my face was mole free. Zap, zap! A medical miracle!

I told myself I wasn't being vain. This was just good health maintenance, I said, but once they were gone, I realized how much those moles had bugged me. I look at pictures of myself, pre-zap, and there, screaming for attention above the right corner of my mouth, is that *huge* mole, and right there above the inner corner of my right eye is that *other* horrible mole. For years, I had been glaring at those two moles, wishing them away. For years, I'd been hiding the larger one behind my hand while I spoke. For years, I'd hated—no, despised—those two "imperfections" on my face. I blamed those moles for everything from bad-hair days to dateless Saturday nights. And now, wonder of wonders, they were gone. I was thrilled.

And I would have remained thrilled forever, but a few weeks after the mole spots had healed, I noticed another spot, just above my lip. It was an old pimple scar. "Never squeeze!" I'd been warned. In a long-ago moment of pre-date weakness, I squoze. The little scar had been there for years, but now it seemed to be getting more obvious. The more I stared at it, the redder and the angrier it got. The moles had been so distracting, I hadn't paid much attention to the scar. Now it had center stage. Was there no end? I made a note to do a little research on the subject of dermabrasion, wondering what Dr. Miracle would charge for a little more zapping.

WHERE DOES IT ALL END?

Where does it all end? Jesus said, "Do not store up for yourselves treasures on earth, where moth and rust destroy, and where thieves break in and steal" (Matthew 6:19). Youth might be a treasure. Beauty might be a treasure. "Moth and rust" could be UV rays and gravity, both destroying that youthful illusion we value so highly. The thieves of time and hot fudge break in and steal away our figures, leaving us wrinkled, faded, and stretch-marked in the dust of their destruction.

"Beauty" may be the legal tender of the world's system, but mercy is the currency in God's economy. God is not concerned with our outward appearance. He sees the heart and offers grace sufficient for all our needs, including the flagging self-esteem and rising self-doubt that aging can bring. He helps us to age gracefully—that is, filled with his grace.

Aging gracefully opens us to receive the gifts of maturity. We can look at the young people around us and realize they are not competition. They're just babies. We know the way they think and act (or don't think and then act, as the case may be). We know what troubles their young minds. How trivial it all seems to us, looking back through the glass of experience. Like looking through the binoculars backward, we find that the gripping concerns of youth seem so small, so far away.

Aging gracefully, we can relax and let youth be youthful, let them run and compete and strive, because we know what they are thinking. They think what we thought at their age. We know how insecure they really are, beneath the swaggering façade. We know they are full of self-doubt about their appearance, despite the fact that they are the most beautiful creatures on earth.

Aging gracefully, we can pray for the next generation. We can encourage the young people in our lives to be a blessing to others by blessing them ourselves. We can show them how to age, full of grace, confident in the Lord. For we've learned (life has proven to us) that, "All men are like grass, and all their glory is like the flowers of the field; the grass withers and the flowers fall, but the word of the Lord stands forever" (1 Peter 1:24–25).

We've come to understand that we are like grass. Beauty and youth are fleeting. Only God is forever. Jesus has the answer. "But store up for yourselves treasures in heaven, where moth and rust do not destroy, and where thieves do not break in and steal. For where your treasure is, there your heart will be also" (Matthew 6:20–21).

May we treasure the lasting beauty of a grace-filled spirit and a heart set on the things of God.

Your beauty . . . should be that of your inner self, the
unfading beauty of a gentle and quiet spirit,
which is of great worth in God's sight.

1 Peter 3:3–4

 **POINTS TO PONDER**

1. Do you know any "beautiful people"? What makes them so?

2. What makes a woman beautiful at twenty? At fifty? At eighty?

3. When have you felt beautiful? Have you ever felt ugly? Describe the experiences.

Uncharted Territory

I told you about that morning I sat in my office, enjoying an extra hour of reading my Bible and talking with the Lord. I told you how I thought, *This is so nice. Such a leisurely morning with nothing to do . . .* That's the morning I was supposed to be at that meeting I'd called. The meeting I'd reminded myself about just the day before. The meeting I totally forgot.

As the hormone war rages, part of the brain (the remembering and organizing part) goes into retreat. This can be embarrassing. This hormonal betrayal, our good sense abandoning us in the middle of a foreign land, this conspiracy against our rational selves, is simply a natural part of aging. It's a passage to be endured, but until fairly recently, it's not been something to discuss.

One of the earliest to break the silence, Gail Sheehy, confessed in *The Silent Passage* that as she neared menopause she was confident she'd "sail right though it." Instead, she revealed, "I veered off course, lost some of the wind in my sails, and almost capsized."

I've read the experiences of other women who were surprised at how early in life the changes became noticeable. How completely unable they were to control what was happening. How helpless they felt. How frustrated they were.

The perimenopause, referring to that time between regular periods and their cessation altogether, is a volatile time. Hormone levels are shifting rapidly. It's usually too soon for hormone replacement. There isn't much to be done, but to endure it. There is good news, however, once the raging subsides. Margaret Mead described a postmenopausal zest that re-energizes life. Countless women report greater satisfaction with relationships, with sex, with creative endeavors, and with themselves, after the hormone wars have ended.

Sheehy says menopause ushers us into a second adulthood, with about as many productive years ahead as the reproductive years we've already experienced. She did the math. Thirty-five years of periods (ages fifteen to fifty). Thirty-five years without (ages fifty to eighty-five).

One woman doctor describes postmenopausal women as "wise oracles of the tribe." I don't know if I'm ready for that, but women across the board report feelings of increased confidence, freedom, and creativity in the postmenopausal years.

Meanwhile, I want a specific map to guide me through the hormonal minefield. I want to see what's coming so I can sidestep the pitfalls. Are there classes I could take, someone who can teach me how to behave as my hair thins and my mustache thickens? Where can I learn how to make the most of night sweats? (I realized, as I cleaned the bathroom at 2:43 a.m., that

I've gotten what I always wanted—an eighth day of the week, except it's at night, two hours at a time.)

The opening for the original *Star Trek* had the line: "To boldly go where no man has gone before." That was revised for the next generation of Trekkies in the name of women's lib: "To boldly go where no *one* has gone before." I'm certainly on a spaced-out trek of my own. I've adopted my own version, for women like me conquering *Menopause: The Hottest Frontier:* "To boldly go where no woman in her right mind would choose to go, but having lost my mind . . . whatever . . ."

Is there a road map for this new frontier? The Bible never actually uses the "M" word, but I think the hormone conspiracy might be implied in some passages. Deborah, for instance, was a strong woman, a leader, and a brave warrior who inspired the army to victory. The general said he wouldn't go to battle unless she came along. Deborah has been described as a "spirited" woman. That might be code for "hormonally challenged." I can get pretty spirited myself at times. Was it a midlife Deborah leading the charge and shouting from the battlefield, "Take that and that and that, you no good, lousy . . ."? If so, that had to feel good.

It's possible that Jael, another woman in the same account (Judges 4:17–22), was also premenopausal. She killed one of the bad guys (she evidently didn't agree with his politics) by driving a tent stake through his skull while he slept. Ouch. Another example of why it's not wise to let "spirited" women handle sharp objects.

In the story of Ruth, we meet Naomi, a widow with an empty nest who finds herself depending on her daughter-in-law, Ruth, also a widow, to take care of her. Is that my future? My daughters caring for me, watching out for me, and supplying my needs? I'd better start being nicer to them.

We've looked at Sarah before, that amazing birth-giving nonagenarian. "Sarah was past the age of childbearing," the Bible says (Genesis 18:11). She was done, finished, dried up. The bakery was closed, the barn locked, the factory shut down. This was a hormonal challenge of cataclysmic proportions. We can understand why she laughed when she heard the news that she was to have a son. She couldn't believe it. She gave birth at ninety. She laughed back then, and lived on to be a good mother. Today she'd be on the cover of the *Enquirer,* appearing on the talk-show circuit, and selling her story to Hollywood to finance Isaac's Harvard education.

But my favorite "old woman of the Bible," the one who provides the clearest road map for me, is the New Testament's Anna. Here's her story:

> There was also a prophetess, Anna, the daughter of Phanuel, of the tribe of Asher. She was very old; she had lived with her husband seven years after her marriage, and then was a widow until she was eighty-four. She never left the temple but worshiped night and day, fasting and praying. (Luke 2:36–37)

Anna was probably a widow for sixty years or so. Her husband died after only a few years of marriage. Life's train carried her down a different track than the one she thought she had a ticket for. She went along for the ride and made the most of the experience.

Anna made a position for herself, worshiping God, praying and fasting night and day. She never quit. She didn't retire at sixty-five. She kept on with her work, praying and waiting for her Messiah. Her dedication was rewarded. She lived to see the infant Christ. She saw Mary, Joseph, and their baby in the temple yard, and "coming up to them at that very moment, she gave thanks to God and spoke about the child to all who were looking forward to the redemption of Jerusalem" (Luke 2:38). She continued to preach Christ. Anna made her own way and she kept going, and going, and going.

Maybe we all must make our own way. We can read what others have to say, sifting through it all to find what matters most to us. We can take good advice when we find it, but in the end, this is a road we travel ourselves. Every woman alive will go through menopause, sooner or later. Every woman's experience will be different. *What* we go through is less important than *how* we go through it. Like Anna, I choose acceptance, I choose purpose, I choose hope.

And I choose joy.

HOPING FOR A GLIMPSE OF GOD

This book-writing business is uncharted territory for me. I once read this advice for writers: "If you want to learn to write, go ahead and write. In the process you will learn how." It's true. I plunged ahead writing this book and in the process, I've been learning how. I'm hoping that the first book is the hardest one to write. It's tricky to find your voice, tricky to learn how to manage your time and your ideas. Tricky to corral those wild mustangs of inspiration.

"Go ahead and write." Practice. Write rough. Write boring, uninspired drivel to your heart's content. Don't be afraid of writing a horrible first draft. Nobody will see it. Just write.

E. B. White said of his writing, "I never know in the morning how the day is going to develop. I'm like a hunter hoping to catch sight of a rabbit." Those rabbits are elusive. I think I spotted one this morning—the grief bunny—but it hopped away, back under the couch before I had a chance to examine it. And later, its cousin—the fear rabbit—galloped through my mind leaving a little trail of raisins that smelled like discouragement and self-doubt. But I went ahead and kept writing anyway.

A woman who was the dean of women at a college was introduced to the new college president—the first woman president in the school's history. The dean, curious to learn the secrets of success, asked her new boss, "How did you ever learn to be a college president?"

The president said, "I haven't learned yet. First, you *become* a college president. *Then* you learn how to *be* a college president."

If I'd asked my mother before I had children, "How did you learn to be a mother?" she might have given me a similar answer. "First, you *become* a mother; *then* you learn how to *be* a mother."

My mother came to help me after my first child was born. For three days, I watched as she fed him his bottles, changed him, and bathed him. She got up with him in the middle of the night, fed him, and rocked him back to sleep. Why? I said

I was in pain and too tired, but the truth was, I was terrified. I'd never even held a newborn baby before, much less had complete responsibility for one.

For three days, I watched as my mother mothered my son. On the third night, when he cried, my wise mother didn't stir. I listened to him cry for a few minutes and then I got out of bed. I picked my baby up and carried him into the living room. I held him close, in a big overstuffed chair, and sang softly to him. He fell asleep. So did I. In the morning, there we were, still in the big chair. He was sound asleep against my shoulder. He was my son. I was his mother, and I began learning how to *be* his mother, from that moment on.

First, you become. Then you learn to be. The answer is the same for my questions today. How do I handle the emptying nest? How can I cope with menopause? How can I learn to be a woman in her fifties, her seventies, her nineties? The answer is always the same. First, you become. Then you learn to be.

There are others who have walked the path before me, willing to share what they've drawn from their own experiences. But the best teacher will be the experience itself. I just have to be brave enough to move forward into it.

That's the hardest part—the fears of what *might* be coming. Will I be healthy into my old age? If I should live a long life, how will I cope with the pain of losing my family and my friends, as my mother has? Will I lose my husband, as my mother has three times and as my older sister has? I don't ask, "How do you learn to be a widow?" I know the answer.

Why borrow tomorrow's trouble? "Do not worry about tomorrow, for tomorrow will worry about itself. Each day has enough trouble of its own," Jesus said (Matthew 6:34).

He's right. Today has enough worry. We can't know the future, can't know what's coming. All we can do is take life as it comes, one day at a time. That's all we get.

If I had known in advance that my first marriage would end in divorce, would I have loved my first sweetheart any less? Would I have held back my heart? No. Would we refuse to become mothers because our children might break our hearts one day? No. Every love of our life will end in pain someday, for us or for others. Do we shrink from love to protect ourselves from the potential pain? No. At least I hope not.

Life is like that rabbit hunt. We don't know how the days, the years are going to develop. We are like hunters, hoping for that glimpse of the wonderful, the surprising, the delightful. I watch for a glimpse of God's gracious hand at work in my life. To understand how his peace settles over me, comforting me in troubled times. To sense the infusion of his courage into my heart, overcoming my fears. To know the truth of his promises—that he is an ever-present help in times of trouble, that he is indeed my refuge and strength (Psalm 46:1).

Life is uncharted territory, an adventure into the unmapped wilderness, an exploration into new frontiers, wild and untamed. Are you scared? I am. How do we learn to lean on God, to trust him, to love him?

We go ahead and lean, go ahead and trust, go ahead and love. In the process, we will learn how.

"No eye has seen,

  no ear has heard,

no mind has conceived

  what God has prepared for those who love him,"

but God has revealed it to us by his Spirit.

1 Corinthians 2:9–10

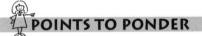

POINTS TO PONDER

1. What's been the hardest change in your life?

2. What do you dread most about getting old? What can you do about it?

3. Who are you today compared to who you thought you'd be?

The Road to Pits-ville

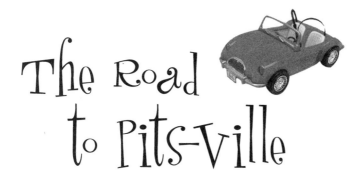

CHAPTER SEVENTEEN

My journal entry for March 2 is just five words: "On my way to Pittsville." That's the day I went to Pittsville, Wisconsin, where I had a speaking engagement. Pittsville is a lovely little city in the middle of the state. Literally. Its latitude and longitude place the town smack dab in the middle of Wisconsin. That's Pittsville's claim to fame. Of course, there is the other obvious connection, which the good-natured residents of Pittsville take in stride, to the idea of being "in the pits."

Looking at that journal entry later, I got to thinking about how many times I'd been "in the pits," how many trips I'd taken down that road to "pits-ville." Too many to count.

Change is hard. I don't need to tell you that. Even changes for the better can be difficult. Families change. Children grow up and need us less and less. It's good that they grow up; it's hard at times to let them. Midlife career changes often bring increased responsibility and the kind of new challenges that would have exhilarated the younger us. Now we can't seem to muster the energy and would rather slow down and smell the roses.

Then there are physical changes. I look in the mirror expecting to see that young girl with the fresh look I used to know. Instead, my mother stares back. Not my young and energetic mother, but my "been through one Depression, two World Wars, and three husbands" mother. The woman in the mirror needs a nap. I haven't had a good night's sleep since the first child got a driver's license. He's almost thirty now. My get-up-and-go hasn't the energy to "got up and went." It's officially dead.

Then there is the expectation that, with all these changes, I'm supposed to finally take time to ponder the deep questions of life: *What's life all about? Why am I here? Who AM I? (I haven't a clue.)*

Once upon a time, I was a competent, energetic, dependable woman who made quick, solid decisions. I was a cockeyed optimist who could always see the positive side of any situation. Now that woman has gone AWOL. I can't blame her. Why would she want to hang around here? All the midlife changes—physical, emotional, mental, family, career, and financial—can be overwhelming. Toss in a few life-threatening medical conditions and it all becomes, as one friend says, "crazy-making."

It's the hormonal changes and the accompanying emotional swings I find hardest to deal with. I wonder, *Are these emotional ups and downs really just a normal part of this life? Or am I actually* (to use the official medical term) WACKO? I'm afraid the answer to both questions might be "Yes!"

My journal tells the story:

"Saturday, 5:14 a.m.: Will I survive menopause? I woke at 2:18 this morning in a hot pool of sweat. Why isn't the pillow ever cool enough? I woke again a half hour later shivering with chills. Half an hour after that, I was flinging the covers off again. Then I felt cold again and curled next to Terry. 'You're too warm,' he said. He didn't believe I was freezing. To him, I was a furnace.

"My brain is collapsing. Its wasp-paper walls are disintegrating. I close my eyes and see a perimeter of twinkling white lights that dim and brighten like fireflies. Do I have a brain tumor? The thought of getting old scares me. I'm sweating my nights away. My head hurts. It's October 21st, and I'm depressed.

"Are hormones running my life? Has my body turned against me? Am I drinking too much coffee or maybe not enough? Maybe I'm just whining too much. Or do I just think too much? This is a bad week for being depressed; I have so much to do. I'm in the middle of painting the family room. The colors are fabulous! I can't do anything about my life, my hormones, or the changes I am experiencing, so I paint and redecorate. I love it, love it, LOVE IT!"

Sometimes the shifts in mood come so fast, I'm amazed I don't get whiplash.

One day I realized that my mood swings and angry outbursts had driven my husband to the end of his endurance. (I'd picked up on his subtle signal. He said, "STOP SCREAMING AT ME! I'M AT THE END OF MY ENDURANCE!") My children were treading softly around me, unsure whether I'd offer them blessings or curses. I was, more than ever, a hormone hostage, and I'd been in the pits too often. That's when I decided to talk to my doctor about drugs.

GOD, THE UNIVERSE, AND MENOPAUSE

My doctor listened patiently as I described what I'd been feeling. I whined on and on. Bless her heart, she didn't bolt from the room. And she didn't offer me any easy answers either. No magic pills. No instant fixes. She assured me that what I was experiencing was a normal part of life. She said these symptoms, often described as PMS, intensify *(Tell me about it!)* as we approach menopause. It was too early to consider hormone replacement and I wasn't real comfortable with that whole idea anyway. We discussed the pros and cons of antidepressants. I wasn't sure I wanted that either.

Then she suggested, very gently, that perimenopause and menopause are most difficult for "those of us who have control issues."

Control issues? Moi? I got a little huffy. *What makes her think I'm a control freak?*

Perhaps it was my being able to tell her that my cycle averaged 26.53 days one year and had lengthened to 28.74 days the next. Perhaps it was the spreadsheet I brought with me, graphing my mood swings. Perhaps it was the bar chart documenting my sleep patterns or the pie chart of my daily weight gain or loss. I suppose she *might* have assumed that a woman who kept such records must like "control."

And I supposed she was right because the feeling of not knowing what was going to happen when was making me crazy. The old signals weren't reliable anymore. I could bloat up at any time. I could lash out without provocation in a flash. Maybe I'd skip this month, maybe not . . . who knew? Certainly not me! No wonder I was in pits-ville!

My God-loving doctor knows me well and she hinted that there were alternatives other than drugs for dealing with my situation. She hinted that it was possible that the God who created the universe, and our bodies, could help a woman deal with the symptoms of menopause.

I thought about that later at home. It sounded good, but was God omnipotent ENOUGH to help ME? I decided it couldn't hurt to find out. I turned to the Bible for answers.

The eighth chapter of the gospel of Luke is packed with action. Here is Jesus calming the storm, raising the dead, and driving out demons. Huge acts of power. Then a woman approaches. She's been subject to bleeding for twelve years. *Twelve years!* No one has been able to heal her. The woman reaches out to touch the hem of his garment. She believes that if she can just *touch* Jesus' robe, she'll be healed. She touches. She is healed instantly. Jesus says, "Daughter, your faith has healed you" (Luke 8:48).

Did I believe that if I would just reach out to Jesus, reach out with just one finger, that a mere touch would heal me? Would it be like Michelangelo's masterpiece on the ceiling of the Sistine Chapel—the picture of Adam reaching his finger toward the finger of God, sparking a divine connection, the lightning of salvation?

I prayed, *Lord, I am reaching out today asking that you would lift me up and out of all this. You know its exact physiology. Lift me out of it, Lord. Heal me. I know it only takes that touch . . .*

I prayed. I waited. No sparks, no lightning. God's answer wasn't going to be instant deliverance in my case. Weeks, then months, passed. My symptoms got worse. I was in the pits more often and felt more frantic about the whole thing.

The writer of Psalm 77 knew what I was feeling. He wrote, "I cried out to God for help; I cried out to God to hear me.... at night I stretched out untiring hands and my soul refused to be comforted.... I groaned; I mused, and my spirit grew faint.... I was too troubled to speak. I thought about the former days, the years of long ago; I remembered my songs in the night" (verses 1−6).

The psalmist tossed and turned, remembering his songs in the night. Did he mean the good old days? I thought often about my own good old days, when the children were little, we were younger, and I felt more alive. Now so often the house felt hollow, and full of echoes. So did I.

The psalmist was afraid, too. "My heart mused and my spirit inquired: 'Will the Lord reject *forever*? Will he *never* show his favor again? Has his unfailing love vanished *forever*? Has his promise failed for all time? Has God *forgotten* to be merciful?'" (verses 6−9, emphasis mine).

I noticed the words: rejected *forever, never* favored again, love vanished *forever,* his promise failed *for all time, forgotten* mercy. I recognized this black-and-white, all-or-nothing kind of thinking. It's the hyperbole of *always, never, forever* that gets me in trouble. "Why am I *always* depressed? Why do things *never* get any better? I guess I'll struggle with this *forever* . . ."

The turning point for the psalmist, and for me, came in verse 10, with the three little words: *"Then I thought . . ."*

Feelings are just feelings. They have no power except what we give them. Thoughts are different. They lead to decisions, and those decisions determine the course of our life. Deciding what we will focus on changes our life. Deciding what we will think about, what we will dwell on, changes the course of the days to come.

The psalmist in despair (verse 6) had thought about the good old days, lamenting the passing of what was once good and joyful. I'd done the same. The psalmist then *decided* to change his focus. He decided to think about and to dwell on God's goodness to his people in the past.

"I will remember the deeds of the LORD; yes, I will remember your miracles of long ago. I will meditate on all your works and consider all your mighty deeds" (verses 11–12).

There is no indication that his *feelings* changed. He set his feelings aside and turned his *mind* toward the truth he knew about God. He decided to *behave* in a certain way, despite how he was *feeling*.

Here's the truth. Nothing on this earth is forever. The bad things are all temporary. "This too shall pass" applies to everything in this life, except for the love of God. I can choose to dwell on all I've lost, all I'm losing. Or I can choose to focus my thoughts on God's consistent love and care for me. I can choose to behave like a woman who is loved and cared for by God, *despite* how I might be feeling at a given moment.

My doctor was right about me. I do like control. I like it, but I don't have it. Nobody does. We only have the *illusion* of control at any given moment. I thought about all the times my life had spun out of control in the past and how God, every time, had showed me his power to reign in the chaos and bring peace.

I knew it was time to acknowledge that I wasn't in control of this latest "change of life." This aging thing was something I couldn't escape, deny, or make "all better." This was something I was just going to have to go through. Certain seasons in life are simply more challenging than others. This was one of them.

I knew that God's plan for my life was ongoing. He had a plan, as always—even now, even with this. I prayed, this time seeking to hear his voice, feel his peace, and sense his assurance. He answered my prayer. He calmed me. He gave me direction.

About that same time, I heard some advice from Dolly Parton that I knew was right: "Pray, and then the time comes when you have to get up and DO somethin'!" It was time for me to do what I knew I should do. I had to start eating better, planning meals and menus more carefully. I needed more sleep; over-the-counter sleeping aids work just fine for me. Walking outside every day lifted my spirits; regular trips up the road in the fresh air work wonders. I knew exercise helped ward off the pits; God has built us to benefit from those natural endorphins.

Most importantly, I started to recognize the first signpost on that road to pits-ville, the first symptom—a feeling, a thought—that I'm heading toward that valley of despair. And I'm learning to ask God for the strength to turn around, to do what I need to do to change course, to direct my thoughts away from the darkness of the pits and focus instead on the bright and welcoming light of his love and care for me.

He lifted me out of the slimy pit, out of the mud and mire;

he set my feet on a rock and gave me a firm place to stand.

Psalm 40:2

 POINTS TO PONDER

1. Describe your personal experience with depression (if any). What did you do about it?

2. Describe a time when you longed for an easy answer to a difficult challenge. Describe the answer, if any, that you did find.

3. What's life all about? Why are we here? Why are you here?

The Revolving Door: Round One

CHAPTER EIGHTEEN

Somewhere between the arrival of my first issue of *Parents* magazine and the first issue of the AARP newsletter, the nest filled and then emptied. Then filled. Then emptied. It seems it's about to fill again. We need a revolving door.

What is going on? What is with children today? What happened to that old pattern: graduate from high school, get a job, finish a four-year degree, get married or *something,* and never come home again? It doesn't seem to apply anymore. Have we made home too attractive? Is the cold, cruel world a little too cold, too cruel for today's young adults?

We're wondering just when we'll experience that *truly* empty nest we've heard so much about. So far, we've had only a taste of it—just enough to whet our appetite for more. But we can't be sure because we didn't have it for long, just for a little while . . . once upon a time . . .

ROUND ONE

I knew my children were growing up when huge tennis shoes sprouted overnight in the front hall, took root, and remained to trip me up. Then came endless showers, morning, afternoon, and evening, forcing us into indentured servitude to the local utility company. Paraphernalia filled the bathroom. Dryers, brushes, curlers, razors, smoothers, and scrubbers. Music blared from every room at once—Christian rock one minute, electric acid something or other the next. The phone began to ring, and ring, and ring. More and more callers. Fewer and fewer asking for Terry or me.

Shortly after that, the family car started disappearing from the driveway, reappearing infrequently and gasless. Once it returned with one headlight hanging from wires. No one had a clue how that happened.

Soon cars began multiplying in the driveway, all models and makes, foreign and domestic, sporting varying patterns of rust and primer. Each had the remains of an engine and tires that once were rubber.

They had another thing in common: they needed fixing, and their "owners" had no money. For a long time, I suspected we had some kind of invisible welcoming sign at the far end of our driveway, inscribed like the Statue of Liberty for Jalopies:

Send us your rusted, your cheap,
Your V−8 engine yearning to belch smoke,
The wretched, rescued from the town junk heap.
Send these—the leaking, sputtering wrecks—to croak.
Our yard light shines upon the pile so deep . . .

Once the shoes and the cars had filled every available space, rumblings of discontent began among the troops, hints they were getting ready to fly. I started making pronouncements. "Once you leave, we'll be converting your room to a home office. Take everything you want to keep. The rest is going in the trash! And take a car and a pet with you!"

They left. One went west, toward the mountains, like a modern-day prospector in search of his fortune, or at least good snowboarding. Another changed majors and moved to the dorm at a new college. The youngest, just after high school, set out in search of herself. They left home. They left behind cars, pets, and trash. And me, sad and lonely, in the middle of the mess.

"They're getting on with their lives," Terry said. "This is what we've been working toward." He was right. We'd set out to give them roots—a place to come from and a sense of belonging to it. We also purposely gave them wings.

"I just never thought they'd actually fly away," I sighed.

"Too bad they couldn't have taken their stuff with them when they flew," he sighed.

OLD DOGS, NEW TRICKS

Things were different at our house with the children gone. I made oatmeal one morning, the usual-sized batch, without thinking. I spent the rest of that day looking for recipes calling for leftover oatmeal—lots and lots of leftover oatmeal. Did you know there really isn't much you can do with leftover oatmeal?

On a Saturday morning trip to the local farmers' market, I bought a loaf of nine-grain bread—the chewy, healthy kind of bread the children always hated. It had no preservatives. I figured Terry and I could finish it, if we dedicated ourselves to the task. We tried. We made toast and sandwiches, and more toast and more sandwiches. We did our level best, but the dog ended up with the second half. She likes mold. My mother said, "Next time, freeze half the loaf." I realized I had a lot to learn.

Being empty nesters had its advantages. I could leave the ironing board up; in fact, it had its own room. Not that it mattered, because we had enough empty closet space to hide a whole month's worth of unironed clothes.

The grocery bill was, for the first time in our parenting life, less than astronomical. Two bagels instead of the jumbo pack, two potatoes, and we could even afford steak—the good cuts! One gallon of milk for the week instead of six. (One day, I poured the last of the milk, soured, down the drain. A first for me!)

One bag of cookies (Why bake when no one is coming home from school to be greeted by the fresh-baked cookie aroma? Sigh.) lasted a whole week, sometimes two. Like our cereal, the cookies had become the grown-up kind—made with whole-grain flour and filled with disgusting things like prunes.

The dog loved us more, sensing we were the only ones around to let her out. I could drive my own car whenever I wanted to. I had a new home office. And a guest room. And another guest room. The house was the same when we came home as it was when we left. We got to bring in our own mail. The phone no longer rang off the hook.

It was quiet. Very quiet. I had lots of time to think about the crazy bygone days of yore. And I cried.

On a coffee mug I bought years ago, a cartoon woman holds a baby in one arm, and a briefcase overflowing with papers in the other hand. She looks frazzled. Her hair is a mess. "I am a working woman," the caption says. "I take care of a home. I hold down a job. *I am nuts!*"

Her shoes are two different colors.

The mug summed up my life and made me laugh for years, in the middle of the tumult of rushing to the office, to day care, to preschool, to the grocery store. Dance lessons, Scout meetings, and the emergency room. The rush and tumble of Christmas mornings. The first days of school and the last days of school. Summer camps and parent-teacher conferences. Band concerts and track meets. Chicken pox. Broken arms and broken hearts. (I get tired just remembering.)

When the youngest was finally in school full-time, I remember standing alone in the house one fall morning. It was suddenly so very quiet. I thought about the previous several years with babies, then toddlers, and finally preschoolers. Those early years that I thought would never end were over and I remember thinking, *Whew! What was THAT? How did I DO that?*

Now another twenty years had flown by, a whirlwind of bumps and blessings. The rush of life, full of activity and obligation, trials and triumphs, had breezed past me, spinning me dizzy and leaving me breathless. And I thought again, *Whew! What was that? Where did the time go? How can it all be over so quickly?*

I missed the kids. I missed the noise. I missed the craziness. I was sorry I hadn't slowed down more often to relish what I had while I had it.

At the farmers' market on another day, I picked up a small bouquet of bittersweet. "It's pretty fragile," the vendor warned me. "Handle it carefully."

Just like life, I thought, feeling more than a little fragile myself just then. At least both my shoes were the same color. Small consolation, but it was something.

> *"See, I am doing a new thing!*
> *Now it springs up; do you not perceive it?*
> *I am making a way in the desert*
> *and streams in the wasteland."*

Isaiah 43:19

POINTS TO PONDER

1. If you have children at home, in what ways are you looking forward to having an empty nest? Are you dreading it? What plans are you making?

2. What's the best part of having little kids around?

3. What advice would you give to a new mother? (If you know a new mother, encourage her. Share your wisdom and perspective.)

The Revolving Door: Round Two

CHAPTER NINETEEN

The old Chevy—packed full with our youngest daughter, Lizz, and all her earthly possessions—disappeared down the street. The nest was finally empty. Terry and I stood on the front step, watching as she drove away. I sniffed and he put an arm around me. He pulled me toward him to offer what I thought would be a word of comfort. He whispered, "Quick! Let's change the locks!"

"No need," I sighed. "The nest is empty for good."

I was so naïve.

Friends with experience in such things said, "They don't stay gone long. They come back. You'll see." Those friends seemed tired. Very tired. And they were right.

Two years later, not just one but two daughters were "temporarily" back home. Katy, in her early twenties, moved home from the dorm to her old room to finish her last year of college. Lizz, then nineteen, came home in the old Chevy after a year out of state "finding herself." (We can only assume she didn't like what she found out there in the cold, cruel world. We found her back at our kitchen table, just in time for dinner.)

What's a parent to do?

It's tough making the adjustment, and re-adjusting, and re-adjusting again to their comings and goings. Part of the challenge is that, when they return home, they bring all their stuff with them. I knew we should have marked it all "No Deposit, No Return"! I'm amazed how much stuff fits in a little Chevy. Almost as much as a dorm room can hold, judging from the piles in our living room.

We'd just gotten our empty nest the way we liked it—neat and orderly. We found some grown-up furniture for the living room, upholstered in fabrics without stain-repellent qualities, designed for adults who can drink a glass of grape juice without spilling. (We don't end up with a purple mustache either.)

Then the girls returned, trailing in their wake boxes of books, tennis rackets, inline skates, guitars, strobe lights, and the assorted components of two—or maybe three (it's hard to tell)—stereo systems. How many woofers and tweeters does one household need?

The whole scene was all too familiar as we stood in the living room, surveying the mess.

"They're baa-ack," Terry said, his voice eerie and wavering, imitating a line from a science-fiction movie.

"It does feel like an alien invasion, doesn't it?" I shivered.

"Well, life does imitate art," he said, picking his way through the debris to a black metal futon, recently crammed into the living room alongside the grown-up furniture. He sat down, sinking lower than he'd sat in years. He looked like a collapsing lawn chair. He gave a little yelp.

"Problem?" I asked.

"No . . . no, I'm fine. This isn't *too* uncomfortable," he squeaked. Being folded in half was evidently interfering with his air supply. He looked around the room. "It sure looks goofy in here."

I sighed. "I think the word is *eclectic.*"

"No, the word is *goofy.*" He shifted forward, then from side to side, grunting as he tried to extricate himself from the futon.

"Problem?" I asked again. This would teach him to be so cocky.

He glared up at me, daring me to laugh at him. "I'm seated . . . ," he said, sounding as old and feeble as possible, ". . . and I can't get up!" We both laughed as I reached forward to help him unbend himself. Futons are made for the young, no question.

The rest of the house looked no better than the living room. Pairs of boots and clunky shoes (bearing an uncanny resemblance to my old "platforms") once again cluttered the front entry. Assorted coats and jackets were once again tossed carelessly over the backs of chairs, inches from the nearly empty entryway closet. (Why IS that?)

The bathroom, when we could get near it, overflowed once again with hair dryers, curling irons, hot rollers, and seven kinds of hair-styling gel, in every imaginable color. Bottles and jars in all shapes and sizes, with names like Root Booster and MegaSpritzer, covered every inch of the bathroom countertop.

"What's 'Bed Head'?" I wondered aloud as Terry and I read labels. "When did it become fashionable to have that 'I just fell out of bed and my hair is a mess' look?"

"When some marketing genius realized kids would pay seventeen bucks for 'Hair Gunk for Cool People.'" He picked up a bottle of Totally Awesome Hair.

"Listen to this," he said, reading from the label. "'Makes a little hair seem like much, much more! Guaranteed!' Hmm." He patted his bald spot thoughtfully. I left the room as he loosened the cap. I couldn't watch.

One thing certainly changed while the girls were away. For years, my girls had made me feel like a walking fashion *faux pas.* "Oooh, Mom, are you really going to wear *that?* In *public?*" "Interesting outfit you've got there, Mom." They'd clip out the Fashion Don't pictures from magazines and leave them where they were sure I'd see them.

While they were gone, it seems I developed style, because suddenly they started raiding my closet. They helped themselves to my "good clothes" and declared open season on my jewelry box.

In many ways, however, it felt just like old times. We had clutter. We reclaimed our place in the supermarket's frequent shopper hall of fame. The utility companies loved us again; lights glowed into the wee hours, the water heater cycled nonstop, and the phone rang constantly. And just like before, it was never for us.

What was hardest to adjust to this time around was the unsolicited advice we were suddenly getting. This was a new development. The tables had turned. Katy lectured me on the evils of simple carbohydrates as I sprinkled sugar on my cereal. Lizz warned me that carbonated beverages would mess up the oxygen molecules in my blood.

Caffeine would kill me, I was told (though my aged mother who drinks potfuls of coffee daily would seem to prove otherwise). If coffee didn't get me, my love affair with dairy fat certainly would. My coffee with real cream—a double whammy—would be my undoing, I was warned. Oatmeal with half-and-half? No-no!

And Lizz, a former carnivore, had seen the light and turned vegetarian. One day, she refused to eat Gummy Bears. Innocent little Gummy Bears?

"What's the problem?" I asked.

"Read the label. They contain animal byproducts," she said.

"Oh," I said. "I thought you were applying your other rule: Never eat anything with a face. By the way, that rule would apply to eating spuds, too, wouldn't it?"

"How so?" she asked.

"You know . . . the Potato Head family?"

She failed to see the humor in that. She rolled her eyes at me. I was just trying to be helpful.

THE END OF A MATTER

We knew this was all temporary. We knew the day was coming when the nest would, again, be empty. We knew why the girls had come home. They'd come just long enough to finish getting their bearings, to reset their compasses. The old model—graduate from high school, get a college degree in four years, and live happily and separately ever after—just doesn't work for everybody. Many children these days need a little extra tarmac before they can take off.

One day, Katy interrupted me as I worked in my home office. "Mom, do you have time for a coffee break?" she asked, and then added with a shy smile, "For some mother-daughter bonding time?"

Some invitations you just can't refuse. Our conversation was peppered with questions—hers for me. "Mom, what do you think about . . . ? Did you ever . . . ? Mom, what should I do about . . . ?" I felt honored. She actually wanted my advice about grown-up issues.

Many such conversations with the girls followed. We talked. We listened. We prayed together, in precious moments grabbed on the fly—moments that were ours only because we were living under the same roof.

Ecclesiastes 7:8 was proving true at our house. "The end of a matter is better than its beginning." Somewhere along the way, we were becoming friends. I savored those days, knowing that one day the children would be ready to take off again and they'd be gone for good. Meanwhile, for a time, God had given us another opportunity to finish what we started—giving them the courage to fly. And we took advantage of the time, adding to the runway, one prayer and one cup of coffee (Okay, fine. Make mine herbal tea!) at a time.

ROUND THREE

The day came when the nest was empty again. Katy graduated from college and was teaching out of state, planning her wedding. Lizz was away at school, living in the dorm, home only briefly during school vacations. Terry and I were getting used to the peace and quiet, to order and freedom, once again. It was nice. Very nice.

One day the phone rang. Lizz was calling from the dorm, two hours away. The last of the children, she's almost, but not quite completely, launched. She chatted awhile about school and life, then just as we were about to hang up, she said casually, "Oh, by the way, did I mention that I want to move home in the spring and finish my degree at the university there?"

So it goes . . . Her room is waiting. I'm glad we didn't change the locks.

> *"For I will pour water on the thirsty land,*
> *and streams on the dry ground;*
> *I will pour out my Spirit on your offspring,*
> *and my blessing on your descendants."*
>
> *Isaiah 44:3*

POINTS TO PONDER

1. If your children have flown the coop, what has helped you most in adjusting to the empty nest?

2. What do you hope your children have learned from living with you? What legacy are you leaving to the significant young people in your life?

3. Write a letter of encouragement to each of your children (or other significant young people in your life). Tell them how much you care, how much you admire who they've become, how proud you are of them.

Wait Training

Do you wait "in" line or "on" line? It depends on where you live. New Yorkers were waiting "on line" long before cyberspace was invented. Around here, we wait "in line." And we don't drink soda. We drink "pop." Soda is that powdery stuff in the orange box that keeps the refrigerator smelling fresh.

My cousin stood in line for over two hours the other day. Was she waiting for tickets to some exciting event? No. Waiting to see an art exhibit or other enriching cultural experience? No. Waiting for a loved one to return from a trip? No. She was waiting to buy doughnuts. Krispy Kreme had finally come to town.

In sixth grade, I waited for a clarinet. I wanted to join the school band but needed to supply my own instrument. We couldn't afford to buy one. My father promised he would rent one from the local music store. I waited.

I'd tried out my cousin's clarinet over the summer. I imagined a clarinet of my own nestled in its case, its sleek black and silver body reclining on black velvet. I imagined putting it together, sliding the cork fittings into each other, twisting the shiny keys into alignment. I could taste the reed's woodiness, pressing the reed to the roof of my mouth with my tongue, testing for just the right pliability. I'd lay that just-right reed against the flat side of the mouthpiece and tighten the screws on the ligature. I'd lift the instrument to my lips, take a breath, and release it, slowly, through the black tube, out across the airwaves, into the universe. Ah, what glorious music we'd make, my clarinet and I.

I dreamed and I waited. My father had promised.

WAITING FOR NORMAL

I was twelve years old, and as I waited for the clarinet, I also waited for puberty. I checked the mirror daily for any sign of the physical changes the books said I should expect. I watched my friends changing, heard their excited whispers.

"Guess who got a bra? Diana!" *How can that be? Diana is only eleven!*

"Guess who started? *Jackie!" Jackie? That stick? Impossible!* Life was just completely unfair.

I was a late bloomer. I waited to "start" until I was fifteen. When "it" finally came, the first time I complained about a cramp my mother said, "Well, this is what you were waiting for. Welcome to the club."

Her tone said it all. *Womanhood is not all it's cracked up to be. It's a long, long time of misery and suffering.* To be honest, I was thrilled to be having cramps at long last, thrilled to be joining the club, thrilled to be "normal." My waiting was over.

Later, I waited for love and for marriage. Waited to finish college, for the Vietnam War to end, for my career to start. I waited for my first child, imagining life with him or her, my sweet, soft baby.

Later, with a houseful of children, I waited for the day they would all be in school. Yet, each May I waited for, looked forward to, the beginning of summer. In August, I dreamed of school starting again and quiet descending. I waited.

I waited for the last one to graduate from high school. I'm now waiting for her to finish college. The nest is empty, sort of. I used to laugh at empty nesters sighing, longing for their children to visit. How pathetic the mothers' plaintive cries: "You never call me! You never visit!" Now I hear a mewling in my own head at times. *I wonder what the kids are doing today. I wish they'd call . . .* One daughter paid me what she called a "pity visit" the other day. I'll take what I can get.

I wait now for menopause, an end to the hormonal storms, to the monthly surprises. I wait for my body to settle into its new mode, a life my older friends assure me is steadier and far less emotionally "interesting." I can't wait to be "normal" again.

LEARNING TO WAIT

We were trained to wait. We said, "Mommy, I'm hungry!" and we heard, "Wait until dinner." We said, "I need new pencils," and we heard, "Wait until payday." Now we're training the next generations to wait.

They say, "A boy wants to take me out." We say, "He can wait until you're eighteen."

They say, "I want to pierce my tongue." We say, "Wait until I'm dead."

They say, "Grandma, I'm hungry!" and we say, "Here, Sweetie! Have a cookie!" (Okay, so things are a little different now.)

We wait for good things, like puberty, love, and marriage. We wait for children, for their first words, their first steps. We wait for needful things—room to breathe, a little peace and quiet. We wait for hard things—the biopsy report, the right moment to break the bad news. We wait for pain to start, and wait for it to end.

We wait.

Recently, I walked into a restaurant just after they opened for lunch, and waited next to the "Please Wait to Be Seated" sign. Nobody came. "Where is everybody?" I muttered. "What's going on here? How long am I going to have to wait?" I complained, huffing under my breath about the inconvenience. (Poor me, having to wait five minutes for a table.)

A lady waiting in line ahead of me turned around and said, "You're going to drive yourself crazy with that attitude, honey. Relax! You'll live longer!"

A just-who-do-you-think-you-are type of comment got stuck on its way out of my mouth. A little voice whispered in my head, *Just who do you think YOU are?* I blushed. I'd just come from a conference where I'd delivered the morning keynote speech. My topic? "Coping with Stress." Ha!

I smiled at the stranger and said, "Thanks. I needed that!" I did.

LEARNING HOW TO WAIT

When my husband and I first moved to our area, we waited for the right jobs. We waited proactively, applying for positions, interviewing and networking, ever alert for opportunities. We waited as our savings ran out, waited as our cupboards emptied. We swallowed our pride and accepted help from friends and food from the local food pantry. We waited for a turn of fortune, for a change of course. A year, then two, and then three. Three long years of waiting.

Somewhere in that process, we decided that it wouldn't matter so much *what* we'd gone through, but *how* we'd gone through it. *How* we waited counted more than *how long* we waited.

Waiting and trusting are two different things. "They that wait upon the LORD shall renew their strength; they shall mount up with wings as eagles; they shall run, and not be weary; and they shall walk, and not faint" (Isaiah 40:31 KJV).

How would we wait? Frustrated, angry, and demanding? Grumbling and huffing? Would we be clinging desperately to God in fear, or would we wait upon the Lord, resting in the hollow of his hand? Which would we choose? Superhuman grappling or supernatural calm?

While we waited, we learned to say, and reminded each other often, "Everything that *really* matters is just fine." And it was true. Everything that really mattered—health, family, God—was just fine.

CLARINET LESSONS

One day a few years ago, a conversation with a good friend turned to the story of the clarinet. I told her how day after day I'd waited, watching through the window as my father came home from work, hoping to see a little black case in his hand. "Maybe tomorrow," he'd say, and later, "Next week, maybe." What he didn't want to say was the truth: we were too poor to buy or rent. There would be no clarinet.

My friend and I agreed there are "clarinet issues" in life. Keeping promises. Explaining truth. Guarding dreams. Nurturing trust. As a parent, I've realized, and so has my family, that God alone is completely reliable. He is the only consistent promise keeper; the rest of us are merely human.

"I wish I'd known that at twelve," I said.

A few days later a package from my friend arrived. Inside was the clarinet she'd played in her school band days, nestled in its little black case, lying against black velvet, sleek and shiny. She'd attached a note: "With Love from Your Father. Romans 8:32: 'He who did not spare his own Son, but gave him up for us all—how will he not also, along with him, graciously give us all things?'"

All things, indeed.

God had already met my deepest need—forgiveness. He'd already showered me with unconditional love, answers to prayer, and, daily it seemed, blessings beyond all I could ask or imagine. Everything that really mattered in my life was just fine.

Now, for no reason other than to say, "I love you," God was giving me the desire of my sixth-grade heart. Rekindling a long dormant dream with a fresh spark of his love, passed on to me through a friend. He'd cared about the girl I was, all along. And he cares about the woman I am now, still watching through the window, hoping, waiting.

And he cares about whatever it is *you* are waiting for today. Trust him. He cares.

> *Do you not know?*
>   *Have you not heard?*
> *The Lord is the everlasting God,*
>   *the Creator of the ends of the earth.*
> *He will not grow tired or weary,*
>   *and his understanding no one can fathom.*
> *He gives strength to the weary*
>   *and increases the power of the weak.*
> *Even youths grow tired and weary,*
>   *and young men stumble and fall;*
> *but those who hope in the Lord*
>   *will renew their strength.*
> *They will soar on wings like eagles;*
>   *they will run and not grow weary,*
>   *they will walk and not be faint.*
>
> *Isaiah 40:28–31*

POINTS TO PONDER

1. What have you waited for? Describe the process of waiting as you experienced it. What or who gave you strength or encouragement while you waited? How was your waiting rewarded?

2. Write a note or make a phone call—don't wait—to someone who has encouraged you.

3. List ten things that are worth waiting for and the reasons they are worth the wait. Which are you waiting for today?

CHAPTER TWENTY-ONE

Real Life

Have you seen those "reality" television programs, where "real" people interact with each other as the camera and crew record it all? Please! Who is ever "real" in front of an audience?

Point the video camera at a kid and you'll get a tape full of mugging, dancing, singing, prancing, and those lovely shots so close-up you can count their nose hairs. Train the camera on the kid's father and you don't know what you'll get: silence and disdain, or mugging, dancing, singing, prancing, and nose hairs.

How many home videos catch me hiding my face behind my apron on Thanksgiving or behind a package on Christmas morning? Then there's me (or at least we think it's me) holding my palm toward the lens to block the view as I duck around the corner. Now *that* is reality programming.

Remember the TV series *Mutual of Omaha's Wild Kingdom* with Marlin Perkins? Did you ever wonder how all that real wildlife just happened to come together in that one spot, all within that one hour? Tigers, hyenas, antelope, monkeys, hippos, and zebras all got a hankering to hit the water hole at the same time? Give me a break.

My keen observation of *real* nature around our house, in our little patch of woods at the edge of the city, has taught me that real nature can be, well, real boring. It takes days for birds to visit, and then only because we've bribed them with food. And they never hang around long enough to pose for pictures. We see an owl once a year, maybe. We've seen a fox once in twelve years. We see rabbits occasionally. We hear raccoons more often than we see them; the devils prefer the cover of darkness for their dastardly deeds.

But if we spliced it all together for a TV special, our back-yard would be as action-packed as the Mall of America two days before Christmas, and just as rough and tumble. Imagine the scene . . .

You hear the voice-over: "And now, from Wisconsin, spon-sored by Mutual of Milwaukee, it's *Wild Suburbs!*" You watch as the owl swoops after the chipmunks and the red-tailed hawk dives after a herd of field mice. Two squirrels squabble over an acorn while the dog goes nuts trying to get out the screen door. The ruckus flushes a flurry of nuthatches, chickadees, blue jays, crows, grosbeaks, and goldfinches from the trees and bushes.

Possums and raccoons waddle through the scene, forsaking their nocturnal habits for the sake of camera time. Watching this, you'd think we'd moved to the African veldt, especially when my husband saunters onto the deck dressed in his dashiki calling, "Has anyone seen my wildebeest?"

A lifetime of exposure to camera tricks and special effects has warped my sense of what's real and what isn't. One night, in a desperate quest for truth, I watched a TV show that promised to reveal to me the "secrets behind the secrets" of certain spectacular magic tricks. The Amazing Bluffo made a whale disappear—an entire whale, tank and all. I was properly amazed. Then I watched as the trick was explained. It was all a sham, an illusion. Just smoke and mirrors. (So this was why they're called "tricks." Hmm.)

I realized at that moment I didn't need the media to mystify me. Life held enough trickery. I'd seen my entire wardrobe disappear into my daughter's bedroom closet, never to be seen again. I'd witnessed, firsthand, vanishing car keys, dissolving hair dryers, and incredible shrinking bank balances.

"Whale, shmale!" I said to the Amazing Bluffo. "I've got my own kind of magic, right here at home!"

REAL LIFE ISN'T ALWAYS PRETTY

Real life, I've discovered, isn't always pretty. I lied to someone the other day, someone who trusts me to tell the truth. I lied to this person, for no obvious reason. There was nothing to gain in telling the lie, but I lied anyway. Afterwards, wrestling with my conscience, I tried to rationalize the lie. I had plenty of excuses, but Jiminy Cricket was having none of them. The truth was simple: I lied.

I don't always lie. Usually, I'm a pretty honest person. I found someone's wallet once in a phone booth. I returned it. I didn't even snoop through it. Well, okay, just enough to find out who it belonged to. I went back to the greenhouse last spring and told them they had only charged me three dollars for a thirty-dollar plant. I gave them the other twenty-seven dollars. I've never accepted too much change at the grocery store. I've never cheated on a test or fudged a resumé.

But I lied. It's so hard to say, "I'm a liar." I can admit to being a truth bender, shaper, modifier, blender, shaver, and enhancer at times. But a liar? Is it "lying" to tell someone who looks like death-warmed-over that they look great? Is it "lying" to tell a child there is a Santa Claus, an Easter Bunny, or a Tooth Fairy? Is it "lying" to tell someone who trusts you that you did what you promised to do, if you didn't really do it? Well, okay, you have me there. I'm guilty. I'm a liar.

I don't look like a liar. I don't have shifty eyes. I don't cast furtive glances hither and yon. I have an honest face. You'd never look at me at the supermarket and say, "That woman looks like a liar." (Well, maybe you would, now that I've confessed all.)

I'm not alone. In one survey, more than ninety percent of adults (most of whom probably have honest faces) said they lie routinely about trivial matters. A third admitted they lie about *important* things. (We'll ignore the obvious question: How do we know these people are telling the truth on the survey?) Assuming the other ten percent who said they didn't lie were lying about *that,* we could use the old excuse: "Everybody does it!"

I can hear my mother saying, "I suppose if 'everybody' jumped off a bridge, you'd jump too?" Mom was right. "Everybody's doing it" doesn't justify what I did.

How did a nice person like me get to be a liar? The Bible says we are sinful from conception. Hard to imagine an innocent baby entering the world with a load of sin, but that's how we are. As

King David put it, "Surely I was sinful at birth, sinful from the time my mother conceived me" (Psalm 51:5).

I used to be in deep denial about this fact of life. I spent years laboring under the delusion that I wasn't so bad; that I had all it took, within myself, to be a decent, kind, honest, caring, and loving human being. And I think I was, for the most part.

But then, out of nowhere, I'd tell a lie, or catch myself hating someone or coveting my friends' stuff. Even if nobody else knew, I knew in my heart I wasn't so "nice." I knew, deep down, the Bible was right about me. Nobody had to teach me to lie or hate or covet. I was sinful from the get-go.

"I am not a sinner because I sin," someone said. "I sin because I am a sinner." This is a deep theological fact of life. It's not my telling of the lie that made me a liar. I told the lie because I *am* a liar. By birth. I inherited the trait—from Eve.

So there's the honest truth. In real life, I am a sinner. But that's not the only truth.

The Old Testament prophet, Isaiah, realized the truth. "Holy, holy, holy is the LORD Almighty; the whole earth is full of his glory." Isaiah's response was to cry out, "Woe to me! . . . I am ruined! For I am a man of unclean lips" (Isaiah 6:3, 5).

When Isaiah admitted that fact, that he was a sinner, he received this assurance of forgiveness from God: "Your guilt is taken away and your sin atoned for" (verse 7). The message was delivered as an angel touched Isaiah's lips with a red-hot coal. *Ouch!*

The truth about me is I am a woman of unclean lips, of unclean heart. I'm a sinner, yet I am invited into the presence of a perfect and holy God whose glory fills the cosmos. How can this be? Because I'm a sinner who has been forgiven. I have this assurance of forgiveness: my guilt has been taken away, my sin atoned for, by the divine fire of Jesus' sacrifice, ignited by the grace of God.

I am a sinner, yes, but by God's grace, I'm forgiven. That's real life.

THE LITTLE THINGS

Real life is in the little things. The crocuses bloom deep purple against the snow. Miniature narcissus fill the garden with deep green and bright yellow despite the frost. Real life is the orioles' call, announcing their arrival in spring, long before we ever see them. We heed the call and nail orange slices to the deck rail.

A Cape May warbler wanders our way, en route to Canada after wintering in the West Indies. How can such a little bird endure such an arduous journey? It stays at our feeder for a week, waiting for the cold air mass pressing down from the north to lift and carry it home. My mother did the same thing after she retired, migrating from Minnesota to Texas each fall, waiting for the cold to recede before venturing back north.

Real life is listening to the floorboards creak overhead, as my husband moves around our bedroom, realizing how silent it would be if his heart problems had been worse. Bypass surgery and the worst of his recovery are behind us. In their wake is a love much deeper than we had before. Heart troubles—any threat to our lives—can be a Godsend. If we let it, fear can teach us to appreciate what we have. How tenuous a hold we have on this life, if we even hold it at all.

Spring came late this year. The cold, dreary, impotent winter days lingered, mirroring our feelings through the long recovery, reflecting our real life. But this morning, the sky is an amazing bright blue through the lacework of new oak leaves that have finally filled in. Now here, at last, is spring's warmth and light.

In real life, I ride a bicycle this spring for the first time in fifteen years. Biking along a road I've previously traveled only by car, I smell lilacs. I slow down and find them hidden in a clutch of pine and poplar. Unexpected lilacs.

My real life is my heart's response to God, overflowing gratitude for all he has done for me. My real life is lived in those moments when I realize how much I need Jesus, and how completely he meets my needs.

My real life is in Christ. The rest of life is just smoke and mirrors. Deceiving. Ever-changing. Disappearing. It's not worth hanging on to. Real life, lived on God's terms, is honest, dependable, and permanent. Jesus' words have been put in this way: "Anyone who holds on to life just as it is destroys that life. But if you let it go, reckless in your love, you'll have [life] forever, real and eternal" (John 12:25, *The Message*).

Real life is the process of moving away from the phony life, where I pretend to be perfectly nice and good. Where I pretend that what matters is my job, my money, and my stuff. Real life is moving away from all that to the place where I can be honestly imperfect. Where I'm not afraid to tell a friend, "I lied to you. Will you forgive me?" Where I tell my child, "I know I've broken your heart. Can we start fresh?" Where I can fall on my knees before God and say, "I'm a sinner, hopelessly lost without you. Please forgive me."

In real life, he will.

> *May the words of my mouth and the meditation of my heart*
>> *be pleasing in your sight,*
>> *O LORD, my Rock and my Redeemer.*
>
> *Psalm 19:14*

POINTS TO PONDER

1. Have you ever told a lie? (Did you just tell another one?)

2. Why do we lie? What do we hope to gain from it?

3. When, if ever, is lying "okay"?

Busy Bodies

CHAPTER TWENTY-TWO

I have a confession to make: I am nosy. I stick my nose into other people's business because I'm curious about what makes people tick—what drives them to do, say, and think what they do, say, and think. This presents a problem since I am not a licensed therapist or cleric. People do not make appointments with me so they can tell me their secrets. In fact, the people I know have begun to clam up in my presence, figuring anything they say could end up in an article or story somewhere.

So, I'm forced to watch strangers in public and make up my own reasons for why they do what they do. For instance, I'm writing this in a coffee shop. A woman at another table is talking with a friend, and she flicks her hair back behind her ear every few minutes. She stares at the table while she talks, avoiding eye contact. Her teeth are crooked. Obviously, she is nervous about the fact that she never got braces. What else could it be?

Later I sit in the parking lot at the grocery store, waiting for my daughter to come out with the goodies I sent her in to buy. A car pulls into a parking slot in the row ahead of me. A woman gets out of the car. She's half my size, wearing white capri pants (when did they stop being pedal pushers?) that hug her well-toned calves.

She has a gorgeous tan. I wonder where she's been for the last decade. Does the term *UV ray* mean nothing to her? Does she want to look like an alligator when she's my age? I look closer. She *is* about my age and shows nary a sign of 'gatoring. She's in great shape. I hate her. I decide she'll be a great villainess in one of my future novels.

She walks toward the store carrying a huge canvas bag. I imagine she'll march right to the gourmet section to shoplift little jars of caviar and olives with pimentos. Since she drives a nice car and wears nice clothes, she must shoplift for the thrill of getting away with it. In my novel, she won't get away with it for long.

Then again, what if she shoplifts because she was raised poor (like I was), and can't get used to the idea that she can now afford to buy anything she wants? Suddenly I feel sorry for her. Maybe in my book, she'll repent and become a nun.

THE FAIRNESS VIGILANTE

Like I said, I'm nosy. I mind other people's business. When I wait in line at the store or the bank, I watch to make sure nobody else is cutting in front of anybody else. I'm the Fairness Vigilante. During the Christmas shopping season, when shoppers are waiting six deep around the cashier counter in the department store, I monitor who was where first. When the clerk asks, "Who's next?" and the guy who showed up most recently jumps forward to say, "I am," I jump in and say, "No, he wasn't! She was here first!" on behalf of the lady who's been waiting even longer than I have. I feel so righteous. What a Good Samaritan I am. Sometimes it's good to be nosy.

While I was in Ecuador, walking through the open-air market, I saw an infant in a wooden box, next to a fruit counter. I wondered where the baby's Fisher-Price baby mobile and the other intellectually stimulating toys were. How were his parents going to raise him to be successful and driven, if they just laid him in a box next to their fruit stand all day?

At the next corner, I watched a toddler sitting in the gutter, picking up grains of sand with her tiny fingers, moving a little sand pile from one spot to the other. Who was keeping her clean and safe? Who was watching out for her future, preparing her for her career, giving her equal opportunity? She went on playing with the sand, the dead insects, and the cigarette butts in the gutter. I thought of my own grandchildren, with all their clean, plastic gizmos and gadgets, enough for a whole troop of little ones like this. Where was the balance?

Later in the market, I watched people buying raw meat that had been lying on the counter in the heat for hours. Hours! I wondered, *Is there no FDA in this country?* Walking down the streets, I tripped over broken sidewalks and breathed ghastly diesel fumes from dozens of buses. *Have they no concept of "emission control"? Where is the EPA? Where's OSHA? Where are all the wonderful government agencies I love to complain about back in the United States? Where are the trial lawyers ready to sue the insurance companies of these negligent sidewalk owners?*

Who's making the rules in Ecuador? Anyone?

It's a burden minding other people's business. It's tiring to always be on the lookout, alert and ever vigilant. And there's another problem: having gathered all this information—or misinformation—what do I do with it? I have a strong need to share it.

It's a fine thing to gather impressions from strangers and create stories for books. That's fiction writing. And it's fine to gather information to lobby for the public good, for child safety, for cleaner air, or for better sidewalks.

But it's quite another story when I take information about other people—people I know—and pass it on. That's called gossip.

That's when my being nosy becomes another thing entirely. That's when I become a "busybody." I'm ashamed to admit that I can be a busybody at times, just like that flock of busybodies in *The Music Man*. Those women spent their days nosing around in other people's lives and then gossiping about it all. The song describes their activities so well: "Pick a little, talk a little, pick a little, talk a little, cheep, cheep, cheep, talk a lot, pick a little more . . ." Like hens around the barnyard, these women clucked their disapproval of what the other chickens were doing, tearing others down to build themselves up. I don't remember when I first heard it, but I know it's true: Big people talk about ideas; small people talk about other people.

Are women more prone to gossip than men? The jury is out on that one, but consider the fact that men use only a tenth of the words women use in a day (which explains why he might be the "strong, silent type"). With that many spare words to use up, it's possible a woman's tongue could, inadvertently, wander into a gossipy area.

THE POWER OF THE TONGUE

Gossip, and the damage inflicted by wayward tongues, is a big issue in the Bible. "The tongue that brings healing is a tree of life, but a deceitful tongue crushes the spirit" (Proverbs 15:4). The truth of that verse came home to me some years ago, while I was going through a divorce.

I don't know anyone who's had an "amicable" divorce, especially when children are involved. Divorce always brings, at some point and to some degree, rancor, bitterness, and pain. I was left living in our family home with my three children, ages two, four, and six.

I hid behind drawn curtains, not opening my window shades for days at a time. One day, I peeked out from behind the curtains and saw a neighbor friend of mine walking to another neighbor's house. I assumed the two women were getting together for coffee. We had all gotten together for coffee many times before. But this time I wasn't invited. I jumped to the conclusion that they were getting together to talk about me and my divorce. The words of Psalm 41 seemed particularly meaningful to me those days. David wrote,

My enemies say of me in malice,
  "When will he die and his name perish?"
Whenever one comes to see me,
    he speaks falsely, while his heart gathers slander;
    then he goes out and spreads it abroad.

All my enemies whisper together against me;
    they imagine the worst for me. . . .
Even my close friend, whom I trusted,
    he who shared my bread,
    has lifted up his heel against me."
(verses 5–7, 9)

David's paranoia and fears were mine. I imagined my friends whispering about me. I withdrew from them; I was certain that whatever I said in confidence, whatever pain I shared, would become the next wave of gossip. My closest relationships became suspect. I withdrew further behind the curtains, deeper into silence and depression.

"A man finds joy in giving an apt reply—and how good is a timely word!" (Proverbs 15:23). My sister-in-law, Jeanette, offered the blessing of that "timely word" to me. She pointed the way out of the darkness for me. She herself had been through hard times, and had been the subject of speculation and gossip. She reminded me of God's love and faithfulness. She became my faithful friend and confidante. She threw me a lifeline. I grabbed it and held on.

I pray I never forget the way I felt in those days. When I'm tempted to gossip, to share the bad news about someone else's life, I want to remember how I felt, standing behind the curtains, alone and afraid. I want to remember the pain of assuming I was the subject of gossip, the imagined betrayal, the aching for a friend I could trust. I don't want to forget how much I needed someone to help me find hope, to help me find my way back into the light.

Jeanette encouraged me to seek professional counseling. When I told that counselor what I'd been feeling, he asked, very gently, "Why did you think you had to go through all of this alone?"

Why indeed?

May I be nosy and mind your business for just a moment? Are you in the dark today? Have life's circumstances left you feeling abandoned, or hopeless, or depressed? Let me ask you that gentle question: Why do you think you have to go through this—whatever it is—all alone? You don't have to. God cares. He's tossing you the lifeline. Grab it.

TONGUE CONTROL

God is serious about "tongue control." James 1:26 says, "If anyone considers himself religious and yet does not keep a tight rein on his tongue, he deceives himself and his religion is worthless."

What good is it if I claim to be a Christian, and express to God a desire to be more like Christ every day, then explode in anger in a bad situation? If I drive around with a fish decal on my car but curse other drivers who get in my way, what good is my religion? If I go to church faithfully on Sunday, but verbally or physically abuse my spouse or children the other six days of the week, what good is my religion? If I quote Bible verses from memory, but blaspheme the Lord's name in frustration, speak bitter words of unforgiveness, or spout bigotry and hatred, what good is my religion?

No good at all. James has more to say about the tongue's potential to cause harm. "Likewise the tongue is a small part of the body, but it makes great boasts. Consider what a great forest is set on fire by a small spark. The tongue also is a fire, a world of evil among the parts of the body. It corrupts the whole person, sets the whole course of his life on fire, and is itself set on fire by hell. . . . With the tongue we praise our Lord and Father, and with it we curse men, who have been made in God's likeness" (James 3:5–6, 9).

God is *very* serious about tongue control, and he wants us to mind our own business. It's for our own good. As Thomas à Kempis says in *The Imitation of Christ,* "We might enjoy much peace, if we would not busy ourselves with the words and deeds of other men, which pertain nothing to us."

I was reading the twenty-first chapter of John's gospel the other day. Peter asks Jesus what's going to happen to John, "the disciple Jesus loved." Peter wanted to know. Was John going to live forever? Was he going to get special treatment, or have an advantage over the rest? Was John going to be first in line at the counter?

Jesus told Peter, not in these exact words, but close: *Mind your own business. What happens to John is my concern.* Then in verse 22, Jesus told Peter directly, "You must follow me."

Jesus says the same thing to me. Never mind what other people are doing. Don't worry about who's minding the church committees, who's making the rules in Ecuador, or who's doing what in the business world. "You, Mary, must follow me."

Follow me.

To this you were called, because Christ suffered for you, leaving you an example, that you should follow in his steps.

"He committed no sin,

and no deceit was found in his mouth."

1 Peter 2:21–22

POINTS TO PONDER

1. Have you ever indulged in gossip? Why do we do it?

2. Have you ever been the subject of gossip? How did it feel? What did you learn from the experience?

3. What is your biggest challenge in controlling your tongue? What can you do to help yourself?

The Things We carry

At a women's retreat recently, door prizes were offered for the three women who carried the most unusual items in their purses. What did the winners offer up? A stuffed platypus, a padded lavender-scented sleep mask, and an empty specimen bottle. I could understand a grandmotherly type carrying a platypus as a diversion. I could understand the sleep mask; I myself never know when the urge will strike to catch a few winks. Hopefully not when I'm driving home from a retreat. But the specimen bottle? How often are we stopped on the street and asked for samples?

I dumped my purse out on the table the other day, partly because I needed to find my library card, and partly because it had been several months and I was afraid something might be growing in there. I was amazed at what I was carrying.

"Treasure hunting?" my husband asked, as I excavated three pennies and a poker chip from the pile.

"More like archaeology," I said, dusting off a bone-shaped refrigerator magnet I'd picked up at the vet's office. I found a wad of unused coupons.

"Here's an expired chicken coupon," I said.

"Isn't that the kind of chicken we always buy?" he asked.

I'm a card-carrying member of a dozen frequent-buyer clubs at our local stores. The video rental shops, pizza places, hair salons, car washes, gas stations, and the deli all have similar deals. "Buy ten, get one free!"

The bakery's Baker's Dozen Club is even better. I buy twelve loaves and I get one free, plus a cookie. A "baker's dozen" deal makes sense at the bakery, but the department store has a Baker's Dozen Pantyhose Club. Buy twelve pairs of pantyhose and the thirteenth is free. Thirteen pairs of pantyhose just has to be bad luck. And I have to wonder if the two stores aren't in cahoots. The more goodies I buy at the bakery, the more I need those control tops. It's a conspiracy.

Every one of these cards has only one hole punched. Every time I go back they ask, "Are you a member?" I say, "Yes, but I can't find my card." They start a new card for me. Someday I'll get my free pantyhose, if I can just find all twelve cards.

The local bookstore offers a discount card for purchases from the children's section. They should just go ahead and call it "The Grandma Club." Buy a zillion children's books and get a dollar off the next one. I love this club. I'm on my tenth card.

Then there's the grocery store's "membership" card. This lets the store track exactly what I buy and when. Normally I'd protest such an invasion of my privacy. But the store gives cardholders like me generous "discounts" on items they've already marked up so they can mark them down, just for me. I'm honored.

Digging deeper into my purse, I found cards proving that my life, health, and auto are insured, that I'm a fair credit risk who is licensed to drive, and the spouse of a retired military officer. Additional cards prove I belong to AARP, several writers' organizations, and the auto club, each with "all rights and privileges awarded thereto." Does this mean I have other privileges coming to me, besides the privilege of paying them my annual dues? I'm really excited now.

Receipts line the bottom of my purse, in case I need additional proof that I'm a gold medalist in the shopping Olympics. It's hard to tell what the receipts are for because they're fading, but these days that doesn't mean they're all that old. Have you noticed that stores are using disappearing ink to print receipts now? The numbers start to fade as I'm leaving the store. This is especially true if I need the receipts for rebates (more of those excellent "marked-up-just-to-be-marked-down" deals). It's tricky to get the rebate form filled out before the receipt disappears. I've been tempted to write on the rebate form, "Trust me. This receipt was for a dozen bags of fertilizer. Please send me my one free bag."

I carry a purse first-aid kit that bulges, not with bandages and gauze, but with makeup. Lip liner and lipstick, eyeliner, mascara, cover-up stick, powder, and blusher—all part of my disguise as a normal person. I especially need the blusher. The ability to blush fades with age. Nothing I do shocks me anymore. Forgetting a meeting has become old hat. Forgetting the children's birthdays, or their names, is no big deal anymore. I have to apply artificial blush to my cheeks so I can pretend to be embarrassed about . . . what was it again? I forget.

Why do I carry eyeliner? The last thing I need to do is draw more lines around my eyes. I might just hang a little sign around my neck. "Don't mock the crow's-feet and the drooping eyelids. Keep breathing and someday this will be you."

Since I carry so much stuff, I bought a purse with little pockets for everything—ID cards, checkbook, credit cards, cash and change, cell phone, and car keys. It even came with a matching umbrella, date book, and eyeglass case. More stuff to carry, and all for $19.99 at the local discount store. This purse could have been the bargain of the decade if they'd only had a buy-ten-get-one-free deal.

THE BURDEN OF DREAMS

I carry all this in my purse, but what else do I carry? An extra twenty pounds. I say "extra," but I don't really know if it is or not. I've carried it for so long, it may be a permanent part of my personal baggage now. I call it "extra" because I have an *ideal* weight in my mind, and it's less than what I weigh today. It's what I used to weigh, when I was the "right" size. It's what I used to weigh when we first moved here, twenty pounds ago when I was forty-one. If I could just weigh that wonderful weight, I'd feel young again. (Take heart you forty-one-year-old readers who are feeling old. Some of us would love to be your age again!) At that dream weight, I don't have the caboose that follows me around now. At that weight, I am young and energetic, beautiful and desirable. In my dreams.

I appreciate the irony that as I write this, there are women for whom my "dream" weight would feel like a ton of excess baggage.

And there are women whose "dream" weight is what I weigh now, or more than that. Think about it, sisters! What are we doing to ourselves? When will we realize that the ideals are not for us real women? When will we get our eyes off the scale and start paying attention to what really matters? (There, I've said my piece. I'll get down off the soapbox. Ahh. I feel lighter already.)

What else do I carry? I carry a notebook and pen so I'm ready to write down thoughts, images, and ideas as they float by. Here's one thought I jotted down: "Move to Colorado." Not on quite the same level as "buy bread." Another note says, "Electrical engineer vs. electric eel = studying vs. living." What's that all about? I must have been watching too much public television.

I carry my dreams. Do I lug them around like a trunk full of elephants? (Sorry.) Do they weigh me down, making me feel like a failure because I haven't achieved them yet? Maybe my dreams are a bouquet of helium balloons. Do I hold onto them with a tight, wet fist, like a child, afraid they'll float away without me? Or worse, that they'll carry me off into space? I'm afraid of heights. Or do I hold them gently and enjoy the incredible lightness of dreaming, confident that the God who gave them to me will also supply the means for their fulfillment. In his time.

THE BURDEN OF THE PAST

I carry the memory of my father, booming and powerful. He loved music and words, loved reading and talking about ideas. He loved poetry. He was also an alcoholic. He looms in my memory, larger than life, filling all the spaces. It was the booze. He was there but not available. He loved, but not consistently.

He took panicky swings at life, trying to be someone, something, needing to live, needing to stop the pain of living.

All the while rejecting the One who could have helped him.

I carry the memory of his love and my longing for more of it. I miss him. He's been gone almost forty years. Does the missing ever stop? There is so much I never got to ask, never got to say. He is so large in my thoughts. Where was my mother?

In one clear memory, my mother and I are sitting on a blanket on the sand at Finn's Point on Cedar Lake, one of several lakes in the city of Minneapolis. It's after supper on a warm summer night, the summer between third and fourth grade for me. The sun is low in the sky. My father and my two brothers are still in the lake. I'm done swimming. My mother shakes drops from a small glass bottle of "Insect Repellent 6–12" into her palm, rubs her palms together, and smoothes the liquid over my narrow shoulders, skinny arms, and scrawny legs. I pull my towel around me and sit beside her, shivering. She pours black coffee from a plaid thermos bottle into its red plastic cup and offers me a sip. We sit together on the blanket, watching the boys play in the water. I take a long, bitter swallow.

Mother is a shadow in the background of our life—ironing, cooking, cleaning, and listening to Arthur Godfrey on the radio. She took good care of us, her hands always at work, her arms holding the family together, providing us a core of sanity in the swirl of alcoholic madness.

For years, I carried childhood pain like a broken arm in a sling. It hampered my forward movement. On every attempt to run, I was forced to slow, clutching my arm to my side, stumbling forward, slower, slower, until I stopped. The wounding stops us if we let it.

Then I met the One who healed me. God offered me everlasting, consistent, unconditional love. Hebrews 13:5, "Never will I leave you; never will I forsake you," were the sweetest words he could have said to me.

THE BURDEN OF TRUTH

What do I carry? I carry on and on about little things, but I carry a big desire to tell the truth about getting older. The truth is, there is a big blank wall we all come to at some point, sooner or later. The wall is there and ugly possibilities are graffiti-sprayed across it. Old age, osteoporosis, menopause, facial hair, sagging muscles, weight gain, heart trouble, arthritis, Alzheimer's, and the rest. Loneliness, poverty, pain.

I came to the wall one day. I couldn't scale it, run around the end of it, or tunnel under it. So I beat my fists against it. "No!" I screamed. "I will not get older! I refuse!" I bought a truckload of vitamin supplements and other products that promised to contain magical anti-aging formulas for my skin, hair, teeth, nails, body, and mind.

What did they do for me? The tooth-whitening product that promised to erase ten years in fourteen days didn't, but it did erase $24.99 from my bank account in fourteen seconds. All these desperate measures made me poorer, but not one second younger. I concluded the obvious: not only was I getting older, but stupider as well. And the wall remained.

Until one day, when I realized that God had *planned* for me to be exactly this age, at precisely this time, and that he had a *continuing* plan for me. I had indeed discovered life after thirty, after forty, and after fifty. Maybe, just maybe, there would still be life after sixty, seventy, or eighty, and even beyond.

And, most importantly, I realized that this life is just the beginning of the eternal life—the "real life"—God promises me. In that moment, the wall fell. Acceptance brought it down.

What was on the other side? Beyond the wall, I discovered space to explore and new things to learn. Beyond the wall, there was time to count my blessings—the comfort of friends, the joy of family, and the satisfaction of service. On the other side of the wall, God kept his promise: "Come to me, all you who are weary and burdened, and I will give you rest" (Matthew 11:28).

Oh, how I'd been burdened, carrying so much for so long. How weary I was of it all. What a relief to let go of all I carried—the stuff of life, the burdens of the past, the worry of the future. What a relief to set it all down and rest. God's promise continues, "Take my yoke upon you and learn from me, for I am gentle and humble in heart, and you will find rest for your souls. For my yoke is easy and my burden is light" (Matthew 11:29–30).

I accepted, gladly, his invitation, and with his promise came peace. Sweet, sweet peace.

> *Praise be to the Lord, to God our Savior,*
> *who daily bears our burdens.*
>
> *Psalm 68:19*

POINTS TO PONDER

1. What weird thing is in your purse right now? Why is it there? (If you're in a group, it's show-and-tell time!)

2. What burdens do you carry? Who gave them to you?

3. God wants to carry our burdens for us. What keeps you from surrendering yours?

Becoming My Mother

I think of Erma Bombeck every time I use a measuring cup. She said she always washed her plastic measuring cups with soap and water after using them, even if all she measured was water. One day it occurred to her how silly it was to do this. Why did she? Because her mother had always done it that way.

I heard a story of another woman who always cut the ends off her ham before baking it. She said she did it because her mother had always done it. Pressed to provide a more logical explanation, she called her mother to find out why.

"Because my roasting pan was so small," her mother explained. "Most hams wouldn't fit."

We absorb so much as we grow. We pass so much along without even realizing it. I can still see my mother ironing in the dining room of our city apartment when I was young. I smell the starchy steam, and remember the long row of crisp pressed shirts hanging from a broomstick propped between two chairs. These were not my father's shirts, or my brothers' shirts. These were the shirts of rich boys whose mothers hired my mother to do their ironing for a dollar an hour. And she was glad to have the work.

Mother stood for hours pressing perfect pleats in those shirt backs. I absorbed, with the steam and starch, the satisfaction of a job well done. Anything worth doing is worth exceptional effort, from brain surgery to bus driving, and yes, even ironing.

The beneficiaries of her dedication cared nothing about the ironing lady or her children. "It's embarrassing," I complained one day over the hiss of steam. "I see this boy in school and know you had to iron his shirt."

"Well, just remember when you see him, that he'd look like a real bum if his shirt wasn't so nicely pressed," Mother replied.

I learned from my mother the value of humble work done well. That there is strength in mustering the inner reserves to do what no one else is willing to do. When my father was too sick with cancer to work, she took a night job cleaning offices in downtown Minneapolis. She hauled home discarded business envelopes and stationery like trophies. One night she came home bearing an incredible treasure: a tape dispenser. There was no shame in scavenging what others had discarded, no embarrassment in reusing castoffs. She was recycling before it was popular.

Now nearly ninety, she excavates the long past like an archaeological dig, wanting to unearth the treasures and share them while she can. She talks about the day in second grade when a boy smashed her only doll—a beautiful porcelain doll she'd received from a wealthy friend. Later that day, during a baseball game where he was the catcher, the boy's nose was smashed by a swing of a bat. As he ran crying from the field, Mother says, "I felt bad, but not too bad." Vengeance is the Lord's but sometimes, it seems, we get to watch.

She talks about the girl who stole her boyfriend. The betrayal crushed her teenaged heart. It still hurts. And there was the time her best friend got mad at my mother and rubbed horse manure in her face as they were walking home from school. "What could I do? She was my best friend. I invited her to my house for doughnuts. My mother always made the best doughnuts."

Her blue eyes still twinkle when she laughs. And she laughs often. She laughs about the day she embarrassed herself in school as she was learning to read. The teacher asked who could identify the word *combed*. Mother eagerly answered, "Come bed!" She had heard her Finnish-born mother say it night after night.

My brother moved from one state to another recently, and Mother was out of contact with him for several days. Meanwhile his birthday came and went. She complained, "He could at least have called on his birthday to thank me for giving him birth." She had gotten him a card, but since she didn't have his address, she couldn't mail it. "I can save it for next year since I haven't signed it yet," she said.

"You could go ahead and sign it," I suggested.

"I'd better not," she said. "I might not be his mother next year."

A LITTLE MORE STRENGTH

My mother started lifting weights when she was eighty-three because, she said, "I need a little more strength." More strength? Three times a widow and at times a single working mother, she's known hardship. She's coped. She always credited her strength of spirit to her Finnish *sisu*—a sheer force of will that guts life out. She'd always claimed she was agnostic, not sure whether there was a God or not. She never read the Bible, never prayed, and never went to church. *Sisu* was always enough.

At the age of eighty-five, she changed her mind. God had been drawing her closer and closer. When a wise pastor explained how she could open her heart to God, she chose to do so. After they prayed together, she said, "Everything is different now. I had an empty feeling, and now it's gone."

Mother looked for eighty-five years and never found anything in this world to fill the emptiness that only God can fill. Her twenty-five-year-old grandson decided to go God's way after hearing her story. "She was my last excuse," he said. "My eighty-five-year-old agnostic grandmother was my last reason for holding out."

Told of this, Mother said, "Thank God he didn't waste his whole life, like I did!" She showed us that it's never too late to change your mind, never too late to accept God's invitation to be his child.

And she prays now. Just as my mother was leaving our home at the end of a recent visit, our dog ran away, disappearing into the woods behind our house. I fumed about this rebellious pup who bolts at every opportunity. I articulated my worst fears. "She'll never come back. She'll get hurt. She'll die out there!"

My mother, familiar with the ways of the prodigal, looked me in the eye and asked, "Where's your faith?" Where was *my* faith? This little woman was suddenly a spiritual giant towering over me. Where *was* my faith?

"I'll pray about this," she said, patting my arm. I felt better immediately. My mother was going to pray. Everything would be all right.

Within five minutes of Mother's departure, the dog was back in the house, happily wolfing her dinner. When I passed along the good news later on the phone, my mother said, "Boy, does God work fast! I was just talking to him as we left your driveway!" As I hung up, the words to an old southern gospel song came to mind: "When Mama prayed, heaven paid attention."

As I iron now, I hear the hiss of steam and smell the starch and I remember conversations with my mother at the ironing board. I remember her advice. Life is about choices. To be content or frustrated is our choice. We can choose to look on the bright side. We decide to expect the best or look for the worst.

I've heard women lament, "Oh no! I'm becoming my mother!" I'm trying to become mine. I see her there in my past, so steady, supportive, and strong. I still feel the scratch of the ironing calluses on her palms, as she stroked my cheeks, comforting me. She still comforts me.

I called her one day to complain about my hectic life; the pressures of career and family and activities had gotten to me. Everything, it seemed, had gone wrong that week. She listened and then said quietly, "But you love that. You get bored when things go too smoothly." A mother's gift—a reminder of who I really am, from the person who has known me longer than anyone else on earth.

I cherish the gift of her laughter, the touch of her hand on my cheek, her prayers for our family. I pray for the courage to continue to work hard doing what's right and what's needed, to hold on to hope, to find the good in everything and in everyone. I pray to be a good wife, mother, grandmother, daughter, sister, and friend. I pray for the humility to admit my mistakes, the grace to forgive myself and others, and the passion to persevere, come what may. I pray to live a life that honors God, being all he has called me to be, every day, at every age.

Why? Because that's the way my mother did it.

> *His mercy extends to those who fear him,*
> *from generation to generation.*
>
> *Luke 1:50*

POINTS TO PONDER

1. Describe your mother (or whoever filled that role in your life). What do you admire most about her (or him)? What have you inherited from that person (by blood or osmosis, positive or negative)?

2. If you have children of your own, or if you fill a "mom" role in someone else's life, what kind of mother do you strive to be? What three qualities are most important for a mother to have?

3. Write a letter to your mother (or that other person) right now, expressing everything you've always wanted to say to them. (It doesn't matter if they are still living or not. It doesn't matter if they ever see the letter. Just write it. Now. For yourself.)

Jubilee

CHAPTER TWENTY-FIVE

God commanded the Israelites to declare every fiftieth year a Year of Jubilee: "Consecrate the fiftieth year and proclaim liberty throughout the land to all its inhabitants. It shall be a jubilee for you; each one of you is to return to his family property and each to his own clan. The fiftieth year shall be a jubilee for you; do not sow and do not reap what grows of itself or harvest the untended vines. For it is a jubilee and is to be holy for you; eat only what is taken directly from the fields. In this Year of Jubilee everyone is to return to his own property" (Leviticus 25:10–13).

I love this idea. Every fifty years, take a break. Declare the whole year sacred. Celebrate. Go home. Would God mind if I had a "jubilee" a little more often than once or twice in a lifetime?

Certainly, every fifty *years* I could benefit from a *real* rest—a whole year off, maybe. (I have a feeling that the second time I get around to doing that, it will be an extremely *long* rest.) What would I do with a year consecrated to God, focused on freedom and rest?

What if I started taking a real rest every fifty *weeks*? A real, honest-to-goodness, two-week vacation each year. Not two weeks cleaning the basement or redecorating the garage but a *real* vacation away from home. A real vacation away from noise and schedules. Away from the telephone, the office, and the bills. (Do I remember how to do that? I hope it's like riding a bicycle.)

What if I declared my own little jubilee every fifty *days* or so? Once every couple of months, I could take a long weekend away. And what if, after fifty hours or so of work each week (isn't that about six days?), I took a day off to rest? Hmm. I could call it the Sabbath! What a concept.

Why wait until the weekend? What if every fifty *minutes,* I stopped to take a little break. A little break to thank God for allowing me to keep breathing. I love that idea! Mini-jubilees throughout my workday.

What difference would it make in my life if I started taking the idea of jubilee seriously?

The Year of Jubilee was the time of being set free from slavery and servitude, the returning of property to its owner, the forgiving of debts. The theme for the year was freedom.

When I turned fifty, I felt a sudden freedom. I realized I would never do all those things I promised myself I would do before I was fifty. I was free from all those expectations of ambitious youth. I admitted I would never be a millionaire or dance on a Broadway stage. I'd never have twelve children and live on a farm with chickens and goats. (Don't laugh. That actually *was* a dream of mine.)

At fifty, my Year of Jubilee, I set myself free.

When I was in my early twenties, I worked one summer at a girls' college run by an order of nuns. One of the nuns, I heard, was celebrating her golden jubilee—fifty years of service to the Lord. Fifty years.

Fifty years was an eternity; I figured it was a miracle the woman could still walk. Then I met her. Over seventy, she was lively and full of mischief. Her laugh was full of life as she passed around pictures of herself on a recent Bermuda vacation.

In one shot, she was wearing a bathing suit. I'd only seen her in her long habit. Not only could she still walk, she swam. And looked pretty good while she was doing it.

She caught me staring at the picture. "Is something wrong?" she asked.

"Sister, you . . . you . . . ," I stammered, trying to think of how to say delicately what I was thinking: that she looked great for her age, that for someone over seventy she was in remarkable shape. Neither sounded like a real compliment. She waited for me to continue. "Well, Sister, you've got LEGS!"

She laughed and said, "Yes, we do, but don't tell the Lutherans!" Then she laughed again. She was free. Jubilee.

My instincts were correct back then. "You look great for your age" isn't such a compliment. It's the "for your age" part that spoils it. The day after I turned fifty, a young woman friend said, "You don't *look* fifty." She thought she was being nice. I told her, "Take a good look, honey. This is what fifty looks like!"

"You don't look _____ (fill in your age of choice)." What does that mean? We have some kind of expectation connected with certain numbers. A certain age is "old." A certain weight means "fat." A certain test score means "dumb." A certain income means "rich." And not one of those assumptions is correct. It's all relative.

A million dollars in cash squirreled away in your mattress hidden from the IRS doesn't make you rich. It makes you a prisoner. Test scores don't determine "smart" or "dumb" in life; they don't measure character or compassion. The same weight can feel awful on the way up the scale, and be a cause for celebration on the way down. And "old" is not a number, it's an attitude. Period.

Set yourself free from your assumptions. Declare your Year of Jubilee!

BIRTHDAY JOURNAL: "FIFTY FEELS FABULOUS"

"All those expectations, goals, wonderings—gone! What do I want to be when I grow up? I am grown up now, and 'I yam what I yam' by default or by design. This is me! The pressure to compete, to perform, is not like it was in my thirties and forties. That drive to impress and to achieve is just not the same anymore. What a relief!

"I wondered what fifty would feel like, to assume the mantle of aging, to cross this threshold. Would I long for yesterday? Would I mourn youth? Fear the future? The reality is none of these. I feel secure, settled, and certain of who I am. Who I wished to be, I have become.

"I am grateful for all the wealth and treasure of fifty years of living, and live in full knowledge that I really have nothing and yet possess everything. Life is a great mystery—a mystery not to be solved, but to be savored. The deliciousness of days parceled out to me one by one, each a gift to unwrap, full of surprise, to be cherished, wondered at. And above all, God— proven so faithful and so fair.

"My Father unchanging, eternal, all wise, and I his child, loved and wholly known. Placed in this time by his design and for his purpose, which continues all the while I draw breath, and beyond. This is fifty. Thank you, Lord!"

Jubilee!

TURN-OF-THE-CENTURY WOMAN

I remember thinking when I was young that I would be about fifty when the century ended. "Turn of the century" has always meant old and ancient. Here I am, a turn-of-the-century woman. Will my great grandchildren think of these times as ancient? Of course.

My grandmother came to America from Finland in 1906, just after "the turn of the century." I turned fifty-one at the turn of the next century. The other day, my E-mail vocabulary builder presented the term *fin de siècle,* a French term "pertaining to the end of the nineteenth century and its climate of sophisticated world-weariness, self-doubt, etc." World-weariness? Self-doubt? That sounded like twentieth, and twenty-first, century thinking to me.

That same day, I read in the book of Isaiah all the prophecies of destruction and God's judgment against Babylon, thousands of years ago. Compared to Isaiah and the eons of history before Christ, and all the history since Christ's time, the 1800s were just yesterday. Yet it seems so long ago.

What were those folks thinking at the end of the nineteenth century, *fin de siècle?* They were probably arguing about whether the new century started on January 1, 1900 or January 1, 1901. They might have wondered how any more progress could possibly be made. The young women probably thought their fashions would be in style forever. Their parents probably worried what the future held for their children.

What were they thinking? The same things the Babylonians were thinking. The same things Isaiah's people were thinking. The same things I think.

They looked up at the same sky I see. The same sky. A hundred years—thousands of years—pass, and it is the same sky.

I have no sense of infinity. I try to grasp it and I start to get a headache. But I know it exists. It's the same with God. I try to understand something—anything—of the vastness of his knowledge and power and I can't. I cannot begin to fathom the unfathomable. He is beyond my understanding, but he is there just the same. Like the sky.

Our perspective is so limited. The breaking news, today's crimes, yesterday's tragedies, and tomorrow's wars may be forgotten in a year. More will have been forgotten in ten years. What is the meaning of this moment? Only the meaning God gives it. Only the accounting I will make for my moments, for my life, when I stand before him. Only that will matter.

What does it all matter in the grand scheme of things? My entire lifetime will only be a drop in the pond, making the smallest of ripples. Why bother?

Because it's my ripple. It may be small, but it's mine. God put me here to make it, and make it I will!

Jubilee!

EXPECTATIONS

"Our egos are always fighting the will of God," our pastor said one Sunday. *Is that the battle that's worn me weary?* I wondered. Was it my ego, resisting this shaping by God into a new woman? Wasn't that what menopause is all about—this "change"?

The "change of life" is a change *in* life, and I resist change. I started out so fearful, panicking at the thought of changing. I tried to deny it was happening. I didn't want to be "old." Then I got very angry. I raged in my journal against the change. All the stages of grieving, I realize now. Grieving for youth. Grieving for what used to be, for what might have been, for what never would be. At the end of grieving came acceptance.

What a relief to learn that this is all a normal hormone-related condition, like pregnancy. (Except in the end you don't have to change anybody's diapers. Well, maybe later.) What a relief to find so much great information these days. We no longer need to suffer alone in silence.

But there seems so little information about how to do this *gracefully*. How do I do this—this metamorphosis—*full of grace?*

My ego gets in the way, not wanting to surrender "who I am": that smart, young, perky, fun girl I've always hoped to be. I emphasize *girl*. I don't want to lose the dream of her. I don't want to turn into the cranky old frump I've always feared was lurking there, just inside my housecoat.

My ego is so concerned with image, with what others think of me, with how I look. My ego is fighting against the will of God, and I've been wounded in the battle.

If God is allowing, even orchestrating, the changes, can God help me cope with them?

A crippled man is healed in Acts 3:1–16: "One day Peter and John were going up to the temple at the time of prayer—at three in the afternoon. Now a man crippled from birth was being carried to the temple gate called Beautiful, where he was put every day to beg from those going into the temple courts. When he saw Peter and John about to enter, he asked them for money. Peter looked straight at him, as did John. Then Peter said, 'Look at us!' So the man gave them his attention, expecting to get something from them."

The man expected to get something from them! Do I expect to receive something from God? And if so, what do I expect to get?

The story continues, "Then Peter said, 'Silver or gold I do not have, but what I have I give you. In the name of Jesus Christ of Nazareth, walk.' Taking him by the right hand, he helped him up, and instantly the man's feet and ankles became strong. He jumped to his feet and began to walk. Then he went with them into the temple courts, walking and jumping, and praising God. When all the people saw him walking and praising God, they recognized him as the same man who used to sit begging at the temple gate called Beautiful, and they were filled with wonder and amazement at what had happened to him."

I imagine Peter and John standing before me, as I am slumped in my depression over getting older. Like this beggar, I have done nothing to "deserve" their help, but I look at these men of God, expecting to get something. Peter says to me, "Prozac and hormone replacement therapy we do not have, but what we have we give you. In the name of Jesus Christ of Nazareth, be uplifted!" They help me to stand, and I start walking and jumping and praising God.

I want to live this way!

When my family and my friends ask me to explain the change in me, I'll paraphrase Peter's words (Acts 3:16) for myself: "By faith in the name of Jesus, this woman whom you see and know has been made strong. It is Jesus' name and the faith that comes through him that has given this complete healing to her, as you all can see."

Freedom. Jubilee!

If the Son sets you free, you will be free indeed.

John 8:36

POINTS TO PONDER

1. What does it mean to "reclaim the Sabbath"? What difference would doing so make in your life?

2. Examine your sleep patterns. (Keep track for a week if you need to.) How much sleep do you need? Do you get enough rest? If not, what steps could you take to ensure that you do?

3. Complete this sentence: "If I had the next year off, I would . . ." (This may give you a glimpse of your heart's desire. How can you move in its direction?)

Free at Last

I rode my blue and white Schwinn bicycle often down the Morgan Hill. It wasn't much of a hill, just a steep rise on a city street—one block of Eighth Avenue North, between Morgan and Newton Avenues. Just one rising block, but to my ten-year-old eyes, it was Everest. I loved to pump long, hard strokes, standing on the pedals, to the top of that hill; the old Schwinn had only one gear. I'd make a slow U-turn in the intersection at the hilltop, and pause. I'd stand astride my bike and survey my domain. All the roads ahead, the empty city lots to explore, all the places I'd never been.

I'd breathe in courage, sit back on the seat, put one foot on a pedal, and push off with the other. Down I'd go, faster and faster, approaching light speed as I barreled down the mountain, my long hair a twitching whirlwind behind me. In that breathless block and a half to our alley, I was a cowboy galloping across Montana, driving wild horses home. I was Amelia Earhart, flying bravely over Borneo. I was an Indy 500 racer, sleek and sure, breaking a hundred miles an hour at least, screaming toward the finish line.

I was free.

PRISON

People make me so mad. They make me mad when they cut in line ahead of me when I didn't offer to let them. People make me mad when they don't offer to let me cut in line ahead of them. I get mad when people cut me off in traffic, or break the traffic rules by tailgating or speeding.

People make me mad when they don't listen to what I am saying, when they make me feel invisible in meetings, in stores, in crowds, or at parties. I get mad when my children don't listen to me. Their eyes glaze over when I start to talk sometimes, or they do some not-so-subtle eye rolling as they exchange glances that say, "Here she goes again . . ." That makes me mad.

Anger is a prison.

Lots of other things have gotten my goat over the years. I was too short to be a model (never mind the "not pretty enough" problem). I was too graceless to be a dancer. My hair has always been too "mousy blah" to be glamorous, despite Raoul's best efforts. I was neither smart enough to get a free ride to a great college, nor rich enough to buy my way there.

My father was an alcoholic. We were poor. Those facts of my personal history will never change. I could choose to let those facts define who I am today. I could choose to see myself as limited by the past, as a long-suffering adult child of an alcoholic.

My father left without saying goodbye. He had cancer. He never told us he had it. One day he just walked out the door and never came back. I saw him a few days later, at his funeral. I was mad at my father for not saying goodbye, and hurt. The past can be a prison. So can its pain.

PRISON IS A CHOICE

Prison is a choice. People can't really "make me mad." I can only allow myself to be angry at things other people do. I can't control other people's actions. I can only control my response to them. I can't change the past. I can only make my choices today, choosing to let the past imprison me or to move on.

We can't control what life throws our way. We can only control our response to life. I'm getting older. I can choose to get old before my time, to dry up and wither on the vine; or I can choose to stay active, alive, interested, and interesting. I can choose to withdraw and feel sorry for myself, or choose to be fully engaged in life.

Why didn't my father say goodbye? This was one of a hundred questions I asked. Literally. I wrote one hundred questions on a piece of paper as suggested by Michael Gelb in his book *How to Think Like Leonardo DaVinci*. Gelb recommended making a list of one hundred questions, as fast as they pop into your mind. They can be questions about anything, from the trivial to the profound. From "When will I clean the refrigerator?" to "What is the meaning of life?"

From the long list, Gelb suggested, identify ten questions you'd like to answer. "Why didn't my father say goodbye?" was one of my top ten. Then, Gelb instructed, instead of trying to give yourself an answer, ask ten *more* questions about each question. I followed his advice.

What I wrote under "Why didn't my father say goodbye?" surprised me. I asked myself, "What makes me think he didn't? What if he did and I just didn't like how he said it?"

I realized that my father *had* said goodbye, in the only way he could. My father was a tenderhearted, sentimental man. He had a poet's soul. How hard it must have been, knowing he was dying, knowing he'd be leaving his wife and his children. How hard to go it alone. How hard to do it without God.

He'd said goodbye in his own way. I see it so clearly now. It was in his angry withdrawal, his depression, and his denial of what was just too painful to face. It was in his eyes—his sad, sad eyes—posing for a last picture with his grandchildren.

How his personal tragedy must have broken his heart. How it broke mine. In asking better questions, I came to better answers. I forgave my father. Forgiving him set me free.

NO MORE WHY-NING!

Here are some of my other questions, and the subsequent questions they inspired: Why is menopause so hard to deal with? (How can I make it better? What resources are out there? Who can help me?)

Why am I so depressed? (How can I be proactive in dealing with my depression? What resources are there? Will exercise help? Will better eating help? When can I get a massage?)

Why is the empty nest so frightening? (What can I do to help myself? What does God have to say in this time of my life? How can I spend more time with him? What have I always dreamed of doing, now that I have some time? What have I learned and where can I teach it?)

In each case, I started with a "why" question. The better questions, the questions that lead toward solutions, don't ask "why." Asking WHY is a dead end. (Stop WHY-ning!) Asking "what, who, where, when, and how" will take me down the road toward answers.

When I started asking better and better questions, the panic to find answers subsided. Have you heard the saying, "When the student is ready, the teacher will come"? The answers come when you ask the right questions, as if the answers have always been there, just waiting for you.

I hope this doesn't sound like that far-out, loosey-goosey, self-help mumbo-jumbo. It's not. Wisdom comes from God. My questions are really my prayers, and God answers, as if he has been waiting, just waiting, for me to be ready to ask.

"If any of you lacks wisdom, he should ask God, who gives generously to all without finding fault, and it will be given to him" (James 1:5). "I will instruct you and teach you in the way you should go; I will counsel you and watch over you," says the Lord (Psalm 32:8).

Help me, Lord. Instruct me. Teach me. Help me understand. Show me the way. Speak to my heart. Heal me. Love me, Lord.

Set me free.

FREE INDEED

I am free in Christ. I heard a radio preacher say that the other day, on the same day I'd read it in the Bible. "It is for freedom that Christ has set us free. Stand firm, then, and do not let yourselves be burdened again by a yoke of slavery" (Galatians 5:1). I heard the same idea later that same week in another sermon and in a song the next day after that. God was trying to tell me something.

Ignorance is a prison. Knowledge of the truth sets us free. As Richard Foster explains in *Celebration of Discipline,* "Good feelings will not free us. Ecstatic experiences will not free us. Getting 'high on Jesus' will not free us. Without a knowledge of the truth, we will not be free." God uses our study of the truth to set us free.

The truth sets us free. Jesus promised it would. "Then you will know the truth, and the truth will set you free" (John 8:32).

The freeing truth is this: it was *for my freedom* that Christ died. He died so that I could be *free* of the burden of guilt, of sin. Free of dread and sorrow. Free of replaying sins in my head and punishing myself, over and over, for my mistakes. Free of regret. Free of worry. Free of the rules, from having to perform to earn his love. Free from the expectations of others—the family, the church, and the world. Free to be the woman God created me to be.

Free in Christ. Free indeed.

NOW

These days, I'm riding a new bike—a "comfort" cycle with two dozen gears and a wide, cushy seat. It has straight handlebars so I won't risk carpal tunnel while riding. Unlike those high-performance racing bikes so popular today, I ride this bike sitting upright. I like that. I never liked the idea of my hindquarters riding higher than my handlebars. This new bike feels more like the old Schwinn. I'm a kid again. Sort of.

I roll down our country road, shifting gears to accommodate the gentle hills, coasting along the flatter stretches. A mile from home, I come to a steeper incline in the road. I have to pedal hard to get to the top, even in the correct gear. The grade counters my efforts. I roll slower and slower as I reach the crest. I stand for a moment at the top of the hill to give my thighs a chance to stop twitching.

Straddling my bike, I stand looking out across the farm fields of the valley that stretches toward home. The sun, setting to my right, casts long shapes of oak trees in some spots and tall corn shadows in others. The land is so peaceful in the twilight.

I adjust my helmet, tightening the chinstrap for a snug, but not strangling, fit. I clean the grit off my sunglasses and settle them back on my nose.

I take a long, deep breath of fresh, cool resolve. With one foot on a pedal, I push off and begin to roll forward, down the steep hill. I quickly pick up speed. Is it a law of physics that a larger body picks up speed faster? Evidently. I worry a little about crashing; I hold on tight to the handlebar grips, not wanting to risk a fracture.

The wind yanks at my hair as it sticks out of my helmet's air vents. I'll need extra conditioner in the morning. Bugs bounce off my sunglasses, off my teeth. I shut my mouth. The wind catches my jacket, billowing it out behind me. I hear the rainproof polyester flapping and snapping. The computerized speedometer on the handlebars reads 7.2 miles an hour. I'm flying!

I've conquered Everest. I've corralled the wild mustangs. I've navigated the skies above Borneo, and now, I'm finishing my race. I'm not setting any new land speed records, but I'm coming in, just the same.

And I'm free. Free at last.

> *Set me free from my prison,*
>   *that I may praise your name.*

Psalm 142:7

POINTS TO PONDER

1. "Ignorance is a prison." "Ignorance is bliss." Which is true and how so?

2. What is holding you captive right now?

3. Jesus said, "Then you will know the truth, and the truth will set you free" (John 8:32). What does it mean to you to be free?

4. Write your own list of a hundred questions. Use them for further "points to ponder."

We want to hear from you. Please send your comments about this book to us in care of zreview@zondervan.com. Thank you.

ZONDERVAN™

GRAND RAPIDS, MICHIGAN 49530 USA

WWW.ZONDERVAN.COM